HIPS, LIPS, EYES & THIGHS

Felicia Bell and Kamilah Asabi

Porchside Publishing, LLC / Plano, TX
HIPS, LIPS, EYES & THIGHS

Porchside Publishing, LLC
P.O. Box 251611
Plano, TX 75025
www.porchsidepublishing.com
Info@porchsidepublishing.com

ISBN 978-0-9838100-2-5
2016957611
10 9 8 7 6 5 4 3 2 1

Acknowledgements

Thank you Lord, Jesus, from whom all blessings flow. Thank you, Kamilah, for suggesting that we leave a written legacy while blood still ran warm in our veins. We did it! To the better parts of me- Ray, Jr. and Feliciti, Mommy loves you.

Love,
Felicia

Who dat said Felicia and Kamilah couldn't do it?! Who dat?! Who dat?! My God, how awesome You are. With every breath and heartbeat, I thank You for allowing Felicia and me to glow in Your glory. To my BFF Felicia, it's been an honor taking this journey with you. To my better half (D), I have much love for you. Thanks Mocha and Latte, my Schnauzers, for burning the midnight oil with Mommy.

Blessings,
Kamilah

Table of Contents

Introduction

Lips, Hips, Eyes and Thighs endeavors to take you on a "real" life journey through the thoughts, feelings, and actions of two BFFs as they reveal life tips, debunk myths, and unveil lies regarding life's indiscriminating teachings. Life lessons told from the soul, undeniable truths their hearts couldn't escape, memories their minds tried to, but could not erase; and words, once spoken, could not be taken away. It's called LIFE- an unbiased certainty that will TKO you if you haven't mastered the skills to overcome its many challenges.

Journey along with Felicia and Kamilah as they, through candid conversations, reveal the ebbs and flows of their lives, past and present, in efforts to help you live your life to the fullest now!

Like diamond discoveries, the duo had to dig deep down to find their hidden treasures- their real value and worth- the substance of what they were made of. Discoveries that took them many years of toiling through dirt, hurt, and much inner work to surface as true gems. And like fine wine, it took time before their true essence could finally be revealed.

What eventually came forth were the most precious jewels that life could birth- priceless and unique. Embodying as their mantra, "What doesn't kill you, makes you stronger," as they took life's bitter with the sweet. In fact, Felicia and Kamilah would have been very ill-prepared for life's long haul if it weren't for the trials and tribulations they had to endure. And like air, they learned that life would always be there- the good, the bad, and the OMG!

Voluptuous lips, a sexy derriere, beautiful hair, and killer hips were said to be Felicia's plus-points. Stunning, intoxicating brown eyes, a magnetic smile, and thunder thighs were Kamilah's. Not to mention her most noted trademark- her walk that was said to make the ground talk.

The BFFs chuckled then, as they do today, when reminded of their so-called birth- brands, which life has taught them mean absolutely nothing compared to what matters- love. Their assets didn't change the naïve little girls they once were, the ladies they became, or the women life is still teaching them to be. From the start, the matters of the heart were always their plus-points, not their hips, lips, eyes and thighs, or other outside stimuli.

In Hips, Lips, Eyes and Thighs, Felicia and Kamilah take you to honest places within their souls; the deep parts, so you can see that life experiences are shared by all. You are not alone and no one is exempt.

Learn, as they have, to shift when life rips them a new one and turn unfortunate experiences into life tips to grow from. That's life! Why meander through life barely surviving until the day you die? You are alive! Be grateful! The possibilities are vast. The future, take hold.

The past, let go. It's never too late to recreate something new. It begins right now and it starts with you.

1.
Life

Life is what it is.
And it ain't, what it ain't!
It happens to us all. We rise.
We fall. That's life!

F

Life is living! Living is through our Lord and Savior, Jesus Christ. Jesus said, "I am the way, the truth the Life...No one can get to the Father but through me." (John 14:6). Life is what you make it. Your life can be beautiful and full of joy. Or it can be dull and full of envy. Which life will you choose to live? I choose the good life. Life is too short for foolishness. Live your life as if it's the last day you have on earth.

K

Life, for the most part has been good to me. I've learned a lot on this journey. Along with age and maturity, I've gained a better perspective on things. I deal with situations better and can instantaneously get people out of my space who don't bring me good energy, regardless of their status in my life.

With the state of affairs today, you often wonder what the world's coming to. I used to live my life in panic, never knowing what tomorrow might bring. Life taught me that it was going to bring what it was going to bring and there wasn't a damn thing I could do about it but live through it the best I could.

I have lost several loved ones over the years. One was a male friend, K.T. Several days prior to his passing, we were totally getting along, which was out of character for us. It must've been a full moon. You would've thought we were arch enemies by the way we argued and fussed over personal philosophies. It had nothing to do with God, of course. It was simply our way of judging and prejudging one another because of different religious beliefs.

K.T. called one evening and said he was going to stop by. There came a knock. And like countless times before, my great nephew (around two years of age) and I raced to unlock the door. Not giving K.T. time to enter, Ty and I high-tailed it back to the bedroom, jumping under the covers in tickled suspense waiting for his entrance. Moments lapsed. Seconds felt like minutes, and minutes, hours. After some time, I knew he must've had a change of plans. Ty had fallen asleep and I was about to join him.

I couldn't wait until the next day. I had some choice words for K.T. for disrupting my sleep and disappointing his little buddy.

The next morning, my childhood best friend, Catherine called and asked if I saw the 10:00 news the night before. "Of course not," I said sharply. Perplexed she would even ask, knowing I go to bed at 8:00 p.m. "K.T. was gunned down last night around 9:00," she announced sadly. My heart stopped. All other bodily functions went hay-wire. I didn't know if I was going to vomit or defecate, or both. But to the restroom I ran, losing all bodily control.

How could that be? I asked myself while trying to control exit flow. K.T. calling me and knocking at my door at approximately the exact time he was murdered. I was grief-stricken in silence for months with only my heart bearing the truth. No one knew of our friendship. We were from different sides of the tracks and headed in different directions.

Ty would often ask where his K.T. was and if he was ever coming to play with him again, which didn't help my grief any. I lost weight and couldn't seem to break out of my funk. It didn't help that I was listening to Michael Jackson's hit "She's out of my life," constantly. As illogical as it sounds, I felt I had to be sad and depressed to validate K.T.'s absence. And so, I was, for months.

At night, my bed would often shake, which was kind of spooky. I knew it was K.T. His spirit was following through on what his flesh could not. But I was not frightened. He adored Ty and me and would never hurt us. I allowed my mom to witness this enigma several times. She would look at me and shake her head, checking it off to my weirdness, I suppose. It, however, showed me that we (humans) were more than our physical bodies. There was also a spiritual component to our make-up as well.

Two distinctively separate conversations with two different individuals changed my life for the better. One, my colleague, Pat came to my office one day out of the blue and said God came to him in a dream and said, "Tell her to let him go. He won't let go of her. So she'll have to release his soul." Right then, Pat and I prayed and the weight of K.T.'s loss was immediately lifted. Soon after, I saw Dr. Cash, a local pastor at a restaurant downtown. When I attended his church a few days later, he recalled that when he saw me in the parking lot of the restaurant, God revealed to him that I had recently lost a dear loved one. He prophesied over me, telling me that God was healing my heart and giving me peace. Once again, prayer lifted my spirit. Not just any prayer; prayer orchestrated from a Higher Source that knew exactly what I needed.

So, life to me is just life. The loss of my dear friend was just part of the circle of life. We live through what we create whether the end result is to our liking. And, sometimes what we create can cause premature death. I believe we are to live our life to the fullest while we are on this earth plane. All of us are born to transform eventually. We don't have to wait until we get to the other side to enjoy the finer things of life either. Live the life you want now! I read somewhere that the definition of insanity was doing the same thing repeatedly and expecting a different outcome. Want different? Do different!

2.
Forgiveness

Forgiveness is giving perspective to life's lessons for the love of you. Let go of whatever the life infraction may have been. Why are you holding on to it like a trusted friend? Release your soul from its emotional control and the pain of the past will lose its hold.

F

Forgiveness is something we must do if we want God to forgive us of our sins (Mathew 6:14-15). Forgiveness is very easy for me. I'm not a person who holds grudges. It's just not healthy. Disliking a person for a wrong they committed hurts you, not them. Because nine out of ten times, they don't even know you are angry at them, or even care.

When you hold strife in your heart it only brings stress, heartache, pain, ulcers, and unhappiness. But if you forgive quickly, turn it over to Jesus; He will work it out for you. People always say, "I can forgive but I won't forget!" Remember, love keeps no records of wrong. If God can forget our past sins when we repent (Hebrews 8:12), then we should at least try to do the same. Don't let the sun go down being angry with a friend (Ephesians 4:26).

K

Forgiveness to me is detaching myself from the incident that caused me the physical, emotional, psychological or social pain in the first place. I see it for what it was, learn what the experience was supposed to teach me, and move on, that much wiser and sharper.

When I was younger, I lived with my grandmother and step grandfather for a short time. I heard the horrors from my mother and other relatives of their life with Dada, as he was called, while growing up. He was said to be mean and ornery.

Growing up, I found this description to be true. He would keep up turmoil and strife, trying to get my brother, Rob and me in trouble any chance he could. After coming inside from a long day of playing, I was hungry and took a piece of meat out of the refrigerator to cook. And yes, I could cook minor dishes as a preteen. The carnivore ended up being steak. This infuriated Dada for some strange reason. He snatched the steak out of the skillet, leaving me standing there drooling. I was pissed to the highest level of 'pisstation'! The nerve of him, I thought as he fussed and cussed me to shame. I was too upset to be moved by his verbal insults, which incensed him even more.

In a matter of seconds, my emotions elevated to his nastiness. I hated him and he could feel it in his bones. He rolled his eyes at me with disdain and I rolled mine back at him. He gestured as though he wanted to hit me. My eyes doubled dared him to. It was about to be elderly abuse for sure.

Just then, my step dad intervened, having seen and witnessed the entire incident. My hunger was later satisfied though I don't recall how. This situation was a pivotal point in my development. I realized at that moment the power of anger and the heights it could reach if not controlled, my emotions being its fuel.

In the case of Dada, my ego took control. Fire met fire and was about to be an inferno up in there. I didn't care much for him anyway. It seemed, in that instant, every unkind thing he had ever done quickly resurfaced, enveloping me in even more rage. Then, for him to act as though he wanted to strike me, oh hell to the no, no, no! Not this day! My stepdad pulled us apart just in the nick of time.

I wish I could say Dada ended up being a wonderful soul. No, he died a miserable, mean, old fart. My life lesson was to understand who Dada was. Once I discovered that truth, the teaching was done. There was nothing left for life to do. It showed me the answer to life's test.

That's why it baffles me when people act as if they can't see the sign posts or hand writings on the wall. Everyone else sees them. Poet Maya Angelou once said, "When a person shows you who they are, believe them." I would add, "Once you know and don't go; the fruit grown, you own." In other words, your mess is a result of ignoring life's lessons, failing its tests.

My grandmother would always say, "A person's ways are their ways and their crosses are theirs, not yours to bear." Who am I to carry someone else's burden? It's difficult enough for me to shoulder my own. So, when negativity emerges from someone's energy field, I just raise my spiritual shield to block the curse. Their negativity isn't mine to own so I kindly send it back where it belongs.

And yes, I've forgiven Dada and others like him many times over. I refuse to allow someone else's outside disposition change who I am on the inside. I have control over my emotional and behavioral thermostat. Like Christie Sheldon, I keep my thermostat at love and above.

3.
Triumphant

If you are breathing, congratulations! You are alive! So why are you just surviving until you die, letting life pass you by? Life is a gift. Cherish it. With each breath, you take, you have the opportunity to create. Rejoice! Lift your voice! Make the choice to be triumphant!

F

Triumphant means to be victorious and successful. The times in my life when I felt like this were when I made cheerleader in the sixth grade, pep-squad in the tenth grade, homecoming court my sophomore and senior years of high school, majorette my junior year, and assistant head majorette my senior year. My other triumphs were when I graduated high school, attended Grambling State University and won Miss Junior. I also graduated Cum Laude from GSU.

I thought I was on top of the world when I got married at age 37. I had a handsome baby boy at age 38, then a beautiful, bouncing, baby girl at age 40. Another triumph came when I did my 1st commercial at Velocity Credit Union and a print work job with Ford. I felt victorious when I modeled for the Banner Bro Show, featured in a magazine, and when my photo was published on a Dudley ad. All that may be fine and dandy, but my real triumph will come when God says, "Servant, well done." (Matthew 25:23) Your name is written in the Book of Life (Revelations 21:27)!

K

People stay stuck in situations, feeling they can't do any better. They realize they are in a rut, hoping for change out in the ether somewhere; never realizing that they are the change that needs to occur. Instead of looking at the battles lost, look at the victories won.

I have started to pay attention to my successes, be they big or small. I realize at this juncture in life that I have much to be grateful for; I am alive, in good health with my mental faculties in check.

It seems people remember your failures and mistakes more so than your accomplishments. Rather, we tend to remember our own errors and missed opportunities more than our successes. And when people, often family and friends, echo them back to us, those old wounds reopen and we nurse them with self-pity. This keeps us stagnant, stuck, in shame or blame, going nowhere fast.

When I was in Junior High School I was coerced by some staff to run for a beauty pageant. I didn't have a dress so my teacher allowed me to use one of hers. Ill-prepared, I didn't win of course. The competition had involved parents that worked over-time, raising money to insure their daughters won. My parents could have cared less and neither could I. I was out of my league, scope of interest. Needless to say, we, the contestants, already knew who the winner was before the curtain opened. I guess they only wanted the rest of us to participate to legitimize the contest.

Anyway, while on stage, I experienced stage fright and forgot my lines. I recall my mother standing up in the audience screaming and shouting at me. I was somewhat devastated. At least I thought I should've been to justify the wave of compassion shown towards me, especially from adults.

However, my mother's outburst felt like home, familiar. Her tone and pitch often miniaturized us kids anyway, there wasn't any need for whippings. I can count the times on one hand that I was ever spanked. Her words were discipline enough.

I stood on stage in a disconnected fog, in awe of all the people in the audience. I corrected my posture, gently wetting my lips with saliva. I had to look the part even if I didn't feel it. Boy did those high heels hurt, I thought, as I absorbed the pain.

A familiar voice from the audience brought me back to reality. It was my older brother, Jack defending me, silencing my mother. My heart began to whimper although my face never showed any sign of defeat. I had mastered that skill of hiding my true feelings as a child, when I'd cry and was told to "shut it up before I give you something to cry about." Like my expressed emotion wasn't enough.

Reality check- this present moment was real, not make believe. I was standing on stage feeling united with my mother as a complete and utter failure. Of course, she never felt that way, but misery loves company. And the misery I felt needed company and she stood out front and center.

Afterwards, some jeered and made fun of me, which served to lower my already fragile self-esteem. I vowed to never, ever enter a pageant again. I was just glad the ordeal was over so I could get out of those damn heels.

Surprisingly, my older brother, Jack was my number one supporter, threatening anyone who thought they would further pounce on my frailness. Needless to say, it was a quiet walk to the car. On the ride home, he reminded me that even though I forgot my lines, I was the prettiest girl on stage. We both burst out in laughter. I was horrible.

I didn't have much to say to my mother for a few days after. I felt the beauty pageant was my moment, regardless of the outcome. And once again, she made it about herself, stealing the show.

Fast forward a few years. I entered the Calendar Girl Pageant while attending college at Grambling State University and won Miss September. I was nervous and wanted to quit. But my silent supporters from the Universe, Angels et al, encouraged me to face my fears and follow through without concern of the outcome. So I enjoyed the moment.

Yes, my mom and other family members and friends were there. My mom beamed with proudness when I stepped onto the stage, beautiful and confident- a reflection of her in live motion. She was a proud Mama. Just having her and others there to support me made me feel like a winner, even if I had lost. Self-worth isn't in whether you win. There's value in just getting in the game.

Not everyone can win. With every victory, there is a loss. That's life! I have made mistakes. But I have many more accomplishments. I hold an Associate in Science Degree in Law Enforcement, Bachelor's Degree in Criminal Justice and a Master's Degree in Social Work. Some people say the helping field is an underpaid, thankless profession. It may be to a degree. But I find joy in helping my fellowman. Its rewards are priceless!

I own my own publishing company and wrote a children's book. I am honored to have co-written this book with my BFF, Felicia. I also started a nonprofit to help 18-25 year olds. I have a wonderful, quaint life, supportive husband, family, and solid friends. I happen to work with people I like. I am in good health, smart, loving and kind. What more can a girl ask for?

When I think about from where I've come, I am humbled and immensely thankful. Love, joy, peace, happiness, health and wealth are now the connections I am eternally linked to. Anything less, isn't God's best for my life. So I purposely make the choice to lift up my voice, rejoice, and be triumphant!

4.
Faith

Faith is knowing that everything that occurs, happens per universal order. So, whatever your fate, know that it'll be okay. In God, truly trust and stand. For not only does He have you in His heart, He has you in His hands.

F

Faith is the substance of things hoped for and the evidence of things not seen (Hebrews 11:1). God says all you need is mustard seed faith (Luke 17:6). Well I'm here to tell you I have a huge mountain of faith. I believe! I know there is a God-Creator of this universe even though I have never seen Him before. Why do I believe that? Because of faith! My favorite scripture is II Corinthians 4:18 – We look not at the things which are seen, but at the things which are not seen. Because the things that are seen are temporal but the things which are not seen are eternal. Nuff said. Can we see Jesus? Eternal. Can we see houses? Temporal.

I have the kind of faith that if I predict it to happen, pray on it in Jesus' name, believe it in my heart and soul, then it will usually happen. Whatever you desire, speak it into the universe. Believe it will manifest. Then, stand back and watch God work. Death and Life are in the power of the tongue (Proverbs 18:21). Whatever you speak will come to past. I am a living witness to this.

K

What people truly believe shows in their personal constitutions. We may try to camouflage our beliefs by being politically correct. But ultimately, who we are and what we truly believe shows up in our daily actions and deeds.

When I graduated from graduate school, it was tough for me to get a job. I applied at endless establishments to no avail. My mother wasn't a religious woman, but she believed in the power of God.

My mom walked to the restroom and got on her knees over the toilet and prayed. The edge of the bed would've sufficed, I thought rolling my eyes. When she reappeared, she told me by 4:00 p.m. that coming Friday I would be employed. "Really now?" I silently asked in sarcasm.

I went to several state agencies only to be left in the lobby, ignored, or avoided by upper management altogether. I was even told by some that they were not hiring. I knew that was a blatant lie because a fellow graduate student had given me the referrals. Then it dawned on me, he was Caucasian and I, African-American. Could that be the deciding factor? I hoped not, but for all intents and purposes, it felt true.

I moped around all week, hoping someone, anyone would hire me. For God's sake, I had a Master's degree. Then Friday arrived. I watched the clock all day, pretending to be as confidant as my mother who was calm, certain that what she asked of God was sure to manifest.

Later that Friday afternoon, I received a call from Chopper, a supervisor from the Louisiana State Office Building, offering me a job as a Child Protection Investigator. She asked if I could come in and sign some papers before the office closed. I said sure and that I would be there in fifteen minutes. I jumped up and down doing the happy dance. I glanced at the clock on the wall. It read 3: 45p.m. OMG! "How did my mom do that?" I asked the heavens.

I have prayed for several things that have yet to manifest. If the truth be told, I don't know if I really expected them to. Prayer to me has always been a good ritual that never actually worked. Sure, some things would come to pass. But not nearly the multitude of things I've asked for over the years. Nonetheless, I keep the faith and pray always. I am still waiting on that million dollars, Lord. I'm just saying (Smile).

Now that I'm older, I cherish every moment of private conversation with the Most High God. Like Jesse Jackson, I keep hope alive. It keeps me in the spirit of great expectation, always open to endless possibilities. This is where faith comes in. The outcome may not be known but the anticipation of a favorable resolve helps me carry on.

I wake every morning and go on with my daily activities- that's faith! I go to sleep at night knowing a new day will greet me the next morning- that's faith! I have choices of what to wear and what to eat- that's faith! I believe in the good of humanity-that takes a lot of faith! (Laugh)

So believe in what you desire to see. And live that truth daily- that's faith!

5.
Love

Love is all of God's magnificence perfectly portrayed on a universal canvas. God's most beautiful artistry captured- you, me, all humanity, everything in air, on land, and sea. Created from the heart of God to just be!

F

Singing…Love in the afternoon. Love is walking in the commandments of the Lord. Love is God. Real love is unconditional. I can truly say that I love everyone! Now there are some people whom I dislike their ways, but I love them anyway. Why? Because God said, "How can you say you love me when you have never seen, when you hate your brother you see every day?" (John 4:20).

It is a must, a commandment to love one another. You cannot enter the kingdom of heaven hating on others. Love your neighbor as thyself (Mark 12:31). If you love

God first, then yourself, then you should have no problem loving others. Even if you say, "they did you so wrong." It's not them that did you wrong, but the disease/sickness they have, that's what did you wrong. Remember, God is love.

K

Love is free. It's the one thing we give and is given to us that supposed to be complimentary. Not so, I have discovered. Love oftentimes comes with conditions, unequally distributed in favor of the dominant in the relationship. I call them Love-Suckers! Like vampires, they extract all your love and then some, never giving any in return.

Most religious teachings teach to love unconditionally. I caution this belief. I believe you should love conditionally and sparingly to protect your love-well. If not, you will be drained and never replenished. Just because they're your mother, father, sibling, spouse or child matters none. If the relationship is love-based, your inner thermometer would be at joy, peace, and happiness. If not, it's not! Again, your insides (how you feel) reflect truth. I'm sorry, but the truth sometimes hurt which is a good thing. God hasn't left us unaware. To me, it's a sin to be a fool or play a fool. Like, we don't have a clue when our inner thermostat has said otherwise. We search for outside guidance, when it's already within, God-given.

From a global perspective, it amazes me just how insensitive some people are, especially the religious and political governances. Just look at the state of affairs in the world today. A lot of the hate and violence have religious and political roots. It makes you wonder what God they are serving. They can be the meanest and nastiest. If one doesn't align with their beliefs or along their party lines and their horns come out.

Okay, correct me if I'm wrong, but God made man/woman in His image. We may have different shapes, colors, and sizes, but all are from the human genealogy just the same. In short, we can tell the difference between a human and an animal by physicality. In regards to behavior, sadly there is sometimes no distinction between the two.

So, if the way we were created was/is okay with God, our Creator, who are we to judge or condemn? God loves, accepts, and values us just the way we are without condemnation. Then, why can't we one another?

While I am on a tangent, let me express another misdeed I see. I don't believe any of God's creation should be destroyed or killed for sport, man's evil deeds, or selfish greed. I don't care what our ancestors said or established as game. It's wrong. When we kill or destroy

God's animal kingdom, we are doing it to Him just the same.

Now back to my point, only an insane person would destroy or kill himself. Yet we do, every time we destroy by word or deed, any of God's children. We are one. What we do to others, we do to ourselves.

I happen to be a pet lover; the owner of two Schnauzers, Mocha and Latte. They love me unconditionally and are appreciative of the care I give to them. They bring me joy, so they are keepers in my Love Circle. Seek out pleasures that can reciprocate the same, that love you back. Love is give and take, a sharing of like energy.

Now the same can't always be said about most human beings. Some people we must love at a distance for our own self-care. They are the ones we love by default because of our history or relationship with them. You may not like my statement but can't deny its authenticity. It is what it is.

We all have that type in our lives. They take and take, never giving in return. Pay close attention to your love-well levels, making sure your joy or happiness hasn't been totally depleted. You'll know for sure after just a few moments in their presence. You began to feel drained or void of positive emotion.

I believe we are all energy beings. If your positive energy isn't fueled enough to withstand negative energy draining, you'll be zapped out quickly. What makes it worse is that they are okay with taking and sucking us dry just as long as we stay in a position to be at their every want and need- the Love-Suckers (Laugh)!

Just remember, love is synonymous with trust and respect. You can't have one without the other. If a person isn't trustworthy or doesn't respect you or your belongings, they don't truly love you. Rather, they are in love with what you allow them to do.

I know people that went to their grave trying to change or make someone love them. Behavior is a choice. People only do what we allow them to. Love them at a distance if you have to, but conserve your love-well reserve. Do it for love's sake!

6.
The Blues

If you're down and feeling blue, gratitude will get you through. Count your blessings. Learn from life's lessons. What you fail to heed, will repeat.

F

Times when you are feeling down, sad, and lonely would bring on the blues. I do not allow myself to get the blues quite often, because when my thoughts try to take me to a sad time in my past, I immediately dismiss it by thinking of happier thoughts.

I also get the blues when a loved one has gone on to glory. Then I think of the fond memories we had together that I'll forever cherish in my heart. I often get the blues when I have a close friend going through a difficult time in their lives. I'll let them know that this too shall pass and for them to keep the faith (2 Corinthians 17:18).

When I think of my failed marriage, I get the blues at times. I know my time will come when I will meet a faithful partner who will love me for me, and not every other skirt he meets on the street.

Other times I'm down when my children are not feeling well. My daughter has eczema and is constantly scratching her skin. My son sometimes has difficulty breathing because of sinus issues. When my children are back to their happy-go-lucky selves, I feel overjoyed. Life will give you the blues. Make sure you have a plan to interrupt the blues cycle. If not, it'll keep you in a funk.

K

When I'm feeling annoyed about something, it's often because I've continued to season it and allowed it to marinate too long. Anger is like an unwanted mutt. It'll stay around if you feed it.

If you live, you will experience the emotional rollercoaster of love/hate and other opposites. Just don't stay in either too long. Have you ever wondered, why you are constantly stuck, wavering, or always falling off the edge? I believe the answer lies in our thoughts, emotions and actions (T.E.A.). We think a certain way and so we become our thoughts, getting stuck in negativity, anger, hatred, doubt, or fear. We become jaded to the nth degree.

We don't need anyone to put us down because we have that skill mastered. We can be our own worst enemies, self-sabotaging any glimmer of hope at the beginning stages. How did we get here?

We are our life experiences, different programs running since conception. We need to pay more attention to the way we feel, our inner thermostat. Our emotions reveal our stagnations. They are our justifiable comforts, our self-nurturing friends. We bask in the positive or negative self-pleasures they bring. In short, we end up being what we're feeling; sad or mad, happy or glad. We begin to see the world from our emotional perspective. We become what we succumb (yield or submit) to.

You can church day and night. Nothing from above will change you from within. You are the change that needs to change, my friend. You can hope your whole life longing for some sort of miraculous intervention to perfect you; when life is always teaching you. What we don't heed (learn and change from), we often repeat (shows up repeatedly).

It is the God in us that is the hope of glory (Colossians 1:27). Stop reading the book (Bible, and other religious teachings) and start being the book! God has fully equipped us to stand. He has breathed life into every child, woman, and man (Genesis 2:7). We have the breath of life. Don't throw in the towel. Yes, you can!

Remember, change occurs from the inside out, not the outside in. Look within for direction and guidance. We know right from wrong innately. That's why we keep our indiscretions, secret-sins private, on the down-low or the low-down.

Start with your temptations- the things you are drawn to and why. A habit is just an appetite that has gone awry. We control how high or low we go. When we know better, we should do better, governing ourselves appropriately. There is no time like the present to change our lives for the better.

I know as grown-ups we can sometimes be very opinionated, lacking boundaries and filters. We sometimes over indulge and play too much. We want everything our way, yesterday. We have yet to learn how to play fair or share.

We also try to cover up our insecurities and self-hatred with phony smiles and unfunny jokes, make-up to conceal what we feel, expensive apparel to dress up our feelings of being down, fancy cars, ego-driven jobs and the like. Not to mention the suburban neighborhoods that make us house poor and side-jokes, called mates that allow us to flaunt or abuse them to inflate our immature, attention-seeking egos.

We think we're being cool, but we are glorified fools. I call it the Blue-Boohoo Syndrome (BBS), faking it until we make it or taking it until we can shake it off. And we've all been there and done that!

Life will always give us the blues in one way or another. None of us is exempt. My grandmother used to say, "Just keep living. Life will one day show up at your door." As long as we live, the blues will always be a phone call, hospital visit, or door knock away. If you don't have the internal wherewithal to handle life's ebbs and flows, you will always stay blue and depressed.

Stop trying to be Superman or Superwoman. They aren't real. They are fictitious characters living in a make-believe world. We are not. Let's keep it real and obtain the skills to be able to deal with whatever life brings our way. There are seasons for everything; a time to be happy and a time to be sad. Remember, blues left unchecked will rule you, causing you to lose in the game of life.

7.
Purpose

Your purpose in life is to love; to give love and receive love. Any other accolades you may receive along life's journey, pales in comparison to your true life purpose- to love.

F

What is your purpose in life? I spiritually feel that my purpose is to serve the Lord, our Father Jehovah and worship Him in spirit and truth (John 4:24). My purpose is to spread the good news about our Lord and Savior Jesus Christ. The good news is He lives and He's coming back for His children to reign in glory with Him for eternity.

My purpose is to also inform you that we have a comforter call the Holy Spirit which was left to lead us and guide us on the straight and narrow path to life and life more abundantly (John 14:16). When we say to ourselves, "Something told me not to do that." That something is the Holy Spirit. Listen the first time, be obedient, make the right choice and you won't have any regrets, disappointments, or bad situations to deal with.

Life can be less complicated if we just trust the spirit of God. My purpose is to also show my children a righteous life so that when they are older, they will not stray away (Proverbs 22:6).

K

You are not defined by your career, bank account, or academic degrees. You are more than a role you chose to play in the life of others. Your purpose is to do what you love (legally), without regrets. Why can't you just be a healthy part of humanity- free, loving, and happy?

I have heard people say our purpose is doing what we love to do. Suppose we love doing a multitude of things? No wonder we are indecisive and are all over the place. I believe you can make anything purposeful by doing it from the heart. God created us unique. We can do whatever we set our minds to do, if we prepare and follow through to completion. Hone in on a field of interest and let your goal be to make it world renown.

When I turned fifty, I wanted to give back. Once you become a half of a hundred, you get a different perspective and outlook. You suddenly realize your latter years may be shorter than your former. You want your remaining days to count for something. So I started a non-profit to help 18-25 year olds get back on track and on a career path. It's been a taxing, yet rewarding journey, but I wouldn't change a thing. My team and I have hearts for young adults, having walked in some of their shoes, and experientially able to forecast their future.

The title Hips, Lips, Eyes and Thighs is symbolic of perceived plus-points, external attributes that many tend to hold in high regard over character and integrity. Like us, our young population must learn that physical features mean nothing compared to the unseen, the matters of the heart- love.

The problem is most of our inner attributes are just as shallow as our outer. Social media has inundated us with images of everything we are not; and everything we should strive a lifetime to be. This mindset keeps us grinding, on a spin-wheel, spinning, hoping for validation, acceptance, or inclusion.

We are too busy trying to be like everyone else that we've forgotten who we are and most importantly whose we are (God's). It's time we flipped the script and returned back to our authentic selves, not continue on this media craze, being robots or puns in someone else's twisted game.

Purpose in life to do what you love. Either love it or leave it alone. If you love more than one thing, just invest equal time in the success of them both, leaving nothing to chance.

8.
Freedom

Everything God created was created to be free. Anything or anyone you feel enslaves you, let them go, lose the control. God has given you peace. Then, peace shall there be. You may love him/her, or even like them too. But when it comes to your sanity and peace of mind, you must choose. There's absolutely nothing wrong with loving/liking someone at a distance, especially if you feel in bondage rather than bonded.

F

Freedom is having peace of mind, not being shackled by the things of life and living in unspeakable joy (1 Peter 1:8). Yes, this is me, and my life. I am free, peaceful, and unshackled because I cast all my cares on Jesus (1 Peter 5:7). Yes, I take all my burdens to Jesus and I leave them there. I don't let anything bother, burden, or worry me. Why? Because, I am a child of the King. My King said He would never leave or forsake me (Hebrews 13:5). Tell me, what does worrying do besides give you ulcers, heart break, and an upset stomach.

If you can fix the problem, then fix it. But if you can't, don't just sit there and worry about it. Give it over to God and don't take it back. Leave it there. The battle is not yours but the Lord's (2 Chronicles 20:15). He can handle it much better than you.

When I was a young child I observed how people handled difficult situations they were in. When I was a teenager, college student, all the way to adulthood, I paid close attention to how people reacted, or what they shared about incidents in their lives. Right then and there, I made my mind up that if a hurtful situation happened to me that I would not react negatively, but in a calm, smart, positive way. So, the majority of the time, this strategy has worked for me.

I'm over fifty now and I still don't let anything or anyone frighten or worry me. Like Kamilah says, "You have to Feel, Deal, and Heal (FDH)!

K

I think we are all pleasers to a fault. We stay in relationships too long, not wanting it to fail. Same goes for a job that doesn't challenge us or support our growth. We are committed to the bitter end; and oftentimes at the cost of our own bitter end. The way you feel is what determines your degree of enslavement. Trust your instinct. Only you can free yourself from your own self-imposed bondage.

Freedom to me is not being in the bowels of debt; feeling shackled, oppressed and beholden to anyone or anything. I felt a sense of freedom when I was no longer under college debt. I must've paid triple what I borrowed in the first place. So like Moses, I went to Pharaoh requesting that he let me go (Exodus 9:1), forgive my college debt because of the overage paid in interest alone. But the Secretary of Education at the time, wrote back saying in essence, "hell no, I'm not going to let your debt go!" (Laugh)

Why are the interest rates so damn high for college students anyway? Is the government on our side? It wasn't until I was in my forties before I paid them off. Sallie Mae had to finally release me and let me go. Hallelujah! Boy, did I do the happy dance! I vowed never to get entrapped again, only to fall prey to the cycle of debt, one credit card after another. I'd pay one off and run two of them back up again. As long as I could afford to pay them, I didn't see anything wrong with continually charging. Easy come, easy go was my mentality. Surely they wouldn't have given me credit cards if I wasn't credit worthy, I ignorantly surmised.

Today, my credit card spending has kept me in an ongoing cycle that I have yet to spin out of. Even though I have excellent credit, I know I shouldn't charge as much as I do. I never charge, however, what I can't afford to pay off immediately. Credit cards to me are a necessary evil that can potentially put you in a world of trouble if you're not cautious.

Only buy what you can afford to pay off, if push came to a shove. Remember the 90-90 rule (90 days to 6 months). If you can't pay it off within this timetable, then don't use credit cards!

For long-term purchases like vehicles and mortgages, of course the above-mentioned principle doesn't apply. But be smart from the start. Have a strategy in place; a contingency plan. Don't leave anything to chance. Your finance is just as important as romance. You want to always be in a position to get it when you need it, even if you have to get it on credit (Laugh).

So, freedom to me is not being in financial debt. What is sovereignty to you? Remember, anything that oppresses or subjugates you, enslaves you. It could be a myriad of things. Just look inside, God has given each of us an emotional thermostat. We can sense when we are not our optimal best. We innately know good, bad, or when something just ain't right. Trust what you feel, knowing God has equipped you with what you need to be happy, at peace, and live your best life now!

9.
Loss

We are born to transform.
Everything has an expiration date.
But you, my love, left too soon.

F

I received the phone call on January 25, 2016, that my baby brother, Lorenza Bell, III died from a massive heart attack. When Tammy, my brother's ex-wife, told me my little brother was dead, I was in disbelief. When I got off the phone, I immediately said to God, "So you took my brother home with you." I stayed calm and then asked my Heavenly Father, "Why so early?" He said, "Because he was ready." I said, "Okay, cool, he's in a much better place with you then in this sinful, worldly world anyway. Now he's my guardian angel."

Throughout my brother's life, he's had several missed encounters with death. If the truth be told, Lorenza should have been dead a long time ago. I once had a dream that he passed. I awoke in torment because my dream was so surreal. Now that my dream has become a reality, I realize how short life is. But it's all good, because to be absent from the body is to be present with the Lord (2 Corinthians 5:8). I know my beloved brother would not come back here if he could. He has his new mansion, streets paved with gold, pearly gates (Revelation 21:21), no more pain and suffering, no bills, just worshipping and praising God on high. No loss, but gain!

K

I've had many losses in my life. The memories still pain me today. I have solace knowing that God knows and loves my loved ones best and in His bosom, they have eternal rest.

In recent years, I felt like my life was on a death marathon. Close relatives were dying in scores. On January 25, 2015, my mother tried to join the ranks. But thank God it wasn't her time to carry the baton. Interesting enough, on this exact same day a year later, Felicia's brother, Lorenza passed away. What's the likelihood?

These ordeals have taught me that death is an integral part of life. As sure as you're born, one day you will transform. I don't think any of us is prepared for the voyage. That's why wholesome, loving relationships are so very important.

Spend time with your loved ones. Make every moment count so when death knocks, you can release them without regret or heavy grief.

Many of my dearest friends have experienced loss as well. My heart goes out to them, especially during celebratory occasions when their loved ones are no longer around. In cases like this, I think we should keep our friends close. Drop them a line or pay them a visit. This is what true friendship requires.

I believe when we leave this physical plane our souls continue in the spiritual realm. There have been many instances in my life where I knew my loved ones were close at hand. We honor them not only in memory, but also when we do good for the betterment of humanity.

So, don't look at loss as something being taken away. We are all here on assignment, for an appointed time and season. And, when our time is up, back from whence we came, we return.

Make this life count for something grand. You are more than your hips, lips, eyes and thighs. What we do for others, we do also for ourselves. All life matters. All of God's creations should be respected and valued.

We worry about the enemy abroad. But really our # 1 enemy is the enemy within. We couldn't do what we do and be okay with it if there wasn't a sadistic spirit at the helm. If our beliefs aren't in alignment with love, then they aren't of God. Period!

Just look around. You can see firsthand what evil can do. What a loss of God's creation. If change doesn't occur, our children will have to bear the burden for generations to come. Right is right and wrong is wrong no matter the cause or justification, most of which have religious or political undertones, I'm willing to bet. Like that's supposed to make wrong, right. I think not!

We should trust our inner-sensor. If it doesn't feel right, it's not! God above is love, and His truth is reflective in everything that is pure and true without exceptions.

10.

Broken Promises

Even with the best intentions, we have no control over the way universal order flows. Do what you can when you can and leave the rest to life's perfect plan. Anything else is out of your control. Promises never made can't be broken.

F

Broken promises are a part of life's journey. Some people do it intentionally and some really mean what they say at the time. I have had many broken promises over my lifetime. Ladies, guys will promise you roses, chocolates, diamonds, mansions just to get your cookies. Don't fall for the "okie-doke!" Tell them: No Finance – No Romance; No Contract – No Contact; No Ring – Nothing!!!

My greatest broken promise to date was my marriage vows. We promised to love one another and stay together "until death do us part." Well, we are both still living, but we are apart, on his account. I'm sure he would say otherwise.

My ex-husband promised me the world, but didn't deliver. I would often ask the Lord, "What did I do to deserve this?" Then I thought about my past sins... You reap what you sow (Galatians 6:7). Nuff said!! That's why it was so easy for me to forgive him for all that he put me through.

You can avoid broken promises by discerning a person's spirit. Listen to a person's conversations when you are dating. Take everything into consideration and do not dismiss anything, even if said jokingly. Don't let love blind you. Ask lots of questions. Go for counseling for at least 3 months. Seek God. Know what you are getting yourself into. It could cost you your life! I thank God every day that mine was spared.

You should be very careful who you choose for a spouse. Remember, marriage doesn't change situations that are already there. Let your yes be yes and your no, no (Matthew 5:37)! Broken promises to our Heavenly Father are also things we must stop doing. We sometimes say, "Lord if you take this pain away, I will never fornicate again until I'm married." Lies! The time you feel better or the urge, you are back at it again. Stop saying things you know you are not going to deliver on. Let your word be your bond (1 John 2:5).

K

Give people a break. Allow them to pause, stop, or change directions if their life calls for it. You only need to be prepared to live strong and move on.

I have had a lot of broken promises. Even I have broken a lot of promises, for which I humbly apologize to any and all I may have offended, known and unknown. Check it off to the girl I was, not the woman I am. I now realize at the end of the day that the only thing with intrinsic value is your word, which holds your character, honor, and integrity at its center.

I was in my mid-twenties, fresh out of graduate school and working as a social worker. My agency attended a social service workshop in Alexandria, Louisiana. Like most professional development workshops, it was boring.

I was approached by this guy with a PhD. *Interesting,* I thought. Although there wasn't much chemistry on my end, I was relieved first and foremost that he didn't have a farm of children by different women. The baby mama drama saga was as real as it gets in my parts. I didn't want the headache or have to expense any of his former indiscretions on my measly social work income. If he had children, I'd love them, but no more than one or two. Past two, I'd have to give him a pass.

His being educated and single were pluses. His being light skinned with green eyes and curly hair, didn't enthrall me any. Being from Louisiana, fair skin with "good hair" (as the ignorant would say) came a dime a dozen. I had a wait to see policy- see how the cards would stack.

As the story, would go, we dated long distance for a few months. I grew to care about him, especially after learning of his life story of heartbreak and struggle for happiness and success. He would often extend himself to help those in need- a quality I much respected and admired.

He lived in New Orleans and I in Shreveport. Because of the distance, we would converse on the telephone for hours. He was the most gentle and kindhearted man I knew. I could see him being my babies' daddy. (Laugh)

He traveled often, calling me in between trips, and bringing me organic souvenirs from his many adventures. On one trip in particular, in early summer, I hadn't heard from him in a while. I became worried. It wasn't like him not to check in. You never knew what might happen to Americans in foreign countries. So my concern was warranted.

It must've of been an angel from above. My mom came into my bedroom with a letter postmarked from one of his many excursions. "Yea!" I screamed like a high school cheerleader. I ripped the letter open. I couldn't wait to hear his sweet whispers of how much he missed me.

As I read, my heart began to beat out of rhythm. My breath escaped me. I fell to the floor, overwhelmed with such emotion that I could hardly sustain myself. His card read: "…I got married. Hope you understand. Have a good life."

"What the f...?" I felt my heart splitting in two. I grabbed my chest, trembling with such intense anguish that I thought I'd die right there. My body reacted to the heartbreak the most, with my stomach knotting and bodily fluids about to explode any second from top and bottom. I didn't know from which end, as this was an unfortunate nervous condition I developed as a child when confronted with imminent fear or loss.

I took hurried breaths, grasping for air to calm down. Finally, I could breathe normally but the tears and sorrow remained. I was no longer *The Great Judger of People* as I thought. I realized right then that even if you do everything right, it could all still go terribly wrong. Other people, I had no control of. At any time, they could change their minds. And, I'd be exposed, left alone, or abandoned.

Life happened to me so unexpectedly. I couldn't have foreseen this coming in my wildest dreams. Nevertheless, it taught me a valuable life lesson- whenever there's a human factor involved, heartbreaks could always occur. You have to be just as vulnerable for potential despair as you are for love.

This occurrence made me cautious for many relationships to come. I felt the need to play chess with subsequent relationships, trying to figure out my opponent's angle, next move. This became exhausting to say the least.

My mother later re-entered my bedroom, finding me crouched down on the floor like a wounded animal. I tried to conceal my hurt. But, the flood gates flew opened as she neared. I didn't want her to know what a stupid daughter she had, even if I was smart enough to obtain a Bachelor and Master's Degree. *How could he be so insensitive and cold? He was a damn psychologist, for God's sake!*

My mom lifted me from the floor onto the bed, wiping the tears and snot from my face. It was humiliating. I was and looked a hot mess. "Dr. Martinez married someone else," the words barely crept out. My mother gently rubbed my back. "He wasn't for you," she said assuredly. "So, God made the inevitable happen sooner than later. Be grateful!"

I guess her words were supposed to make me feel better. Maybe they would have tomorrow, but not today. I just wanted to wallow in misery, as if I deserved to for trusting and wanting to be loved by him. I was a game he played. I wondered how his new wife would feel if she had known about me. *Could there be others?* And as life would have it, I eventually found true, amazing love. If I hadn't had to sift the wheat from the tares (Matthew 13:24-30), I probably wouldn't have appreciated the find.

It took a while to get my bearings back. But eventually I did. And yes, he called a few months later with the BS apology. I had a list of choice expletives, but I kept the conversation honorable. My mama definitely raised me better than that!

When I finally stopped feeling sorry for myself and re-evaluated the situation, I had to admit that my mom was right. There were plenty of tell-tale signs that I shouldn't have ignored. And of course, I had plenty more broken promises since. But, who's counting! (Laugh).

So, my humble advice to you is to never, ever settle for a supporting role in someone else's life script. If you aren't the lead, leave. If your partner doesn't want only you, let him or her go. If they show you signs of their untrustworthiness, be grateful, even if it foils your life plans. Life is about the journey, including all the ups and downs. And, as I'm sure you've learned by now, life isn't always smooth sailing.

11.
Me in 3D

There are many sides of you. You like many things. We are multi-dimensional beings. Don't let people put you in a box. You are not the sum total of your mistakes or indiscretions. Learn the life lesson and continue to grow and learn more life lessons.

F

3-D to me is pure transparency. It's the revealing of your true self without being fake or phony. I am the sweetest person you'll ever meet in life. No one is a stranger to me. I treat everyone the same. All men are created equal in my eyes, even though we are not all treated equal. I am the kind of person who doesn't want to hurt anyone's feelings or mistreat anybody. I'm a people pleaser. I hate to tell people "no." I used to try to accommodate people, even if it made me uncomfortable, which is not good. I have since grown. I know how to express and defend myself.

I consider myself a very loving person. Not only do I want the best for myself, but others. I'm not a jealous or selfish person either. If I have it and you need it, I'll let you borrow it. I love the Lord with all my heart, soul, body and mind (Matthew 22:37). He is the head of my life. I live my life to be a holy example for others. In short, that's me in 3-D!

K

People think they know you by your past, what you've done, your so-called life transcript, if you will. Like, you are only your past. But as long as you're in the land of the living, there will always be battles lost, victories won. The beautiful thing about life, however, is with every heartbeat, breath, there are new beginnings.

Never let your story end. Write new novels daily. Experience the many faces of you, happily doing everything you've ever wanted to do. I heard Bishop T.D. Jakes once say that people often put periods behind your name. I concur. It is as if they compartmentalize you into categories that their skewed vision can only see or believe you to be. So like thieves in the night, they steal or shoot down your dreams.

My dad had in his heart to name me after his great aunt, Mildred Marie, born in the late 1800s or early 1900s, I presume. Aunt Millie was said to be a protector of the community, marrying in her later years, never having any biological children, raising my dad, her great nephew, as her own. People who know me know where I am going with this.

Although I never met Aunt Millie, I knew instinctively as a child that my dad gifted me with her embodiment, everything she was and all she meant to him. I was told that she was like a mother to him and that he absolutely adored and worshipped her. Her passing, as you can imagine, was a great loss.

OMG! What a banner to have to carry; a generational heirloom that I never asked for or ever wanted the responsibility of. Whatever emotional contract my dad made with my birth name, his first daughter, was made with prejudice and without my consent. Vette, Keja, and Sarah, be thankful that you all were later arrivals.

As the story, would go, I confided to my mother as a child that I felt cursed. Not understanding spirituality then as I do now. Something just wasn't right. I didn't quite feel like myself. Of course as a child, I didn't have the terminology. However, I felt I lived under some type of spiritual cloud of sort. There was always a mist of sadness and depression in and around me, even with the brightest smile and seemingly successful life.

Like my Aunt Millie, I married later in life, didn't have biological children, raised my great nephew, was a social worker and considered a matriarch of the family. Do you see the similarities?

As a child, my dad would often stalk me, watching me play and follow me from afar. I could see him out of my peripheral. "What the hell?" I'd think to myself. My stepmother would tell me to ignore him. His overprotectiveness was exhausting, although I knew he meant well.

My dad later confessed that he had a premonition that one of his daughters would be violently murdered. He had been living with this torment since my birth. But it wasn't me. It was my sister, Angela, and her unborn son, who died at the hands of her partner when I was eighteen, in the early '80s.

My name was later changed to *Kamilah Asabi*. *Kamilah* means the perfect one. Perfection being the crown I strive for. It keeps me on my Ps and Qs. *Asabi* means born of a select birth. Just the mere fact I was born, amen and amen.

I have met a lot of people who were namesakes too, and like me they ABSOLUTELY HATED IT! They wanted their own name, and not have to be linked to a memory, family tradition, or have to live under the legacy of dead relatives. No disrespect.

With age and maturity, I cleared the fog that seemed to surround me throughout my early development and address this issue head-on, releasing its perceived attachment to my soul. With certain memories, however, this feeling of *something-ness* would resurface. I'd just remind myself of who I was, and whose I was and the emotion would vanish instantly. Was it a generational curse or blessing? Who knows? Who cares? I just knew how it made me feel, uncomfortable. And it seemed to linger until I learned to stand in my own light.

My simple advice to parents - STOP comparing children with other people and their likeness! We aren't them! Let your children be their own unique self, even if they possess similarities to other folk. God made us individuals, in His image, not theirs. It's enough to live our own life, than have to also live out the memory of others and their emotional attachment to you.

Like you, I'm multifaceted, holding many titles and positions. To know me, is to like or love me. You get to pick. Life has taught me that I am more than a name, past shame, future accomplishments, or mistakes. I am multi-dimensional, 3D. It's definitely more to me than my hips, lips, eyes and thighs. What about you?

12.
The Test

As long as you live, life will throw many challenges your way. Remember, the small obstacles only appear to gear you up for life's TKO (Trials/Knowledge/Opportunities). Life is always teaching and preparing us.

F

Sometimes I believe God puts us to the test, to see if we will follow Him or others. Our teachers/instructors give us tests to see if we have comprehended what they've taught. Our parents put us to the test to see if we have learned over the years what they have instilled in us. When we get our driver's license, we have to take a written and driving examination to see if we are qualified to be behind the wheel.

Most people must take tests to pass to the next level, to graduate high school/college, or to get that job promotion. Some people put their mates to the test to see if they are the one! A few people put their spouses to the test to see if they still love and care for them. Most students put their teachers to the test to see how angry they can make them act in class.

Life is a huge test we are taking to be successful in this world. Will you pass the test, or will you be left behind?

K

I'm sure, like me, you've had many life tests. What doesn't take you out, will take you to higher levels of maturity and responsibility. With each day comes new challenges to conquer, lessons to learn. Life is simple. If we don't like what we're getting, stop participating.

To tango, you need a partner. Watch who or what you choose to partner with. Choose wisely. Just because it may give you momentary pleasure, its co-requisite can be a lifetime of pain.

Remember what we fail to heed, we repeat. It keeps showing up in our lives. And whatever that like may be, our "need radar" has summons it. Don't believe me? Get an urge and watch it surge. Heat rises. Fire will connect with its likeness. That's why it's called wildfire. (Laugh). It can be an unruly beast. And you thought that he/she came into your life just because? Haven't you heard the saying, "You attract what you are."

Your subconscious is all about the real you. And your ego will make your truth come true. Subtleness to extremes, we'll do whatever it takes to turn dreams/fantasies into reality. We keep that little black book handy, just in case; maintain certain relationships to keep us in the game. Not to mention Facebook or other social media outlets to keep the lines of interest opened for wires to someday cross, get intertwined. No mystery there.

So, the life test I'm referring to is about ex's and other acquaintances. My experiences have been that ex's that keep the lines of communication open only do so to test the authenticity of their ex- partner's new relationship. They hone in on the solidness of your new bond, looking for any signs of cracks.

Any communication, other than an occasional hello, outside of your marriage or committed relationship is cheating, unless there are children involved. Reality check! You aren't that awesome that your ex still wants you. Don't be a fool! That's probably why you are the ex because you are so easily manipulated. And by privately staying in contact with them, you are proving them right.

You may wonder how I am so knowledgeable on the subject. Uh, I use to be the ex that they kept in touch with, confided in. And yes, it inflated my ego every time they would contact me to tell me their problems. I'd think, Thank God it's her and not me. Of course I knew it was a ruse to get me back, which was never going to ever happen. I move forward, never back.

I have heard people say, "but we're just friends." BS! Wish your old friends well without using South Central Bell (Laugh)! Pray for them if you have to. Send them good thought energy if you must. But don't stay in contact with ex's, especially if your husband/wife/partner isn't included in on the private texts, calls, lunches or dinners. Be transparent. If there isn't anything to the re-established friendship, text or call him/her in the presence of your husband/wife/partner. Can I get an amen?

Furthermore, why are you telling them your problems anyway? Talk to your significant other or attend counseling, but never ever disclose your private affairs to anyone other than the involved party.

If my husband and one of his exes happen to cross paths, I'm okay with them having casual conversation. It's life. I am too old to trip over what I can't control anyway. I am not with him 24/7 and neither is he with me. This is where trust and respect comes in. He knows my stance on the subject and I, his. We share whenever we've talked to whomever from our past. We do it out of respect for one another, which is our responsibility, not our ex's. Enough said.

Also, watch your other relations as it relates to your union. They often inquire about your love-life, but secretly cheer any indication of problems or unhappiness. I heard Floyd Mayweather refer to them as subliminal haters. They smile and appear to wish you well, but really don't. Remember, your success may reflect weaknesses in them, especially if they have low self-esteem or their relationship is void. There isn't anything you can do about it. That's their issue to deal with, not yours.

So never wonder why or how you keep getting into certain situations. Whatever you keep flickering will eventually become a flame. And fire attracts fire. With every life test, you will either elevate or disintegrate. Trust your inner thermostat. Always do a self-temperature or an awareness check. Know where you are and what you're doing at all times. Heat rises. So protect yourself.

13.
The Scare

The scariest moment in life is when the outcome is beyond our control. Just know you can always go to God. He is our rod to lean on. Strength, when we're not strong. Whatever the situation, remember God reigns. We may have a broken heart or bruised ego, but still alive all the same.

F

The scare is when I'm frightened about something and about to panic. As a child, scary movies really thrilled me, especially watching them alone and in the dark. Afterwards, I was terrified for at least 3 days, but I could not stop watching horror flicks, even though they made me very intense and afraid.

Another scare in a woman's life is the possibility of being pregnant by a man who means her no good. The biggest scare for a human being is to receive the bad news from their doctor telling them they have a terminal illness, with only a few months to live – to get their house in order.

The greatest scare for a misbehaving child is when a parent tells them, "Just wait until we get home!" Most children start crying at the anticipation of the punishment! Just as your heart races prior to the big drop on a roller coaster ride. Whatever the scare may be for you, trust God. I am a living witness that He will be your rock, fortress and deliverer in the time of trouble (Psalm 18:2).

K

We must face life's situations head on. You can't heal what you're not willing to feel. Deal with it. FDH-Feel, Deal, Heal! Put it into perspective. Check it and move on. Remember, life happens to us all. No one is exempt!

A few years ago, I had a scare after a routine mammogram examination. It was the look on the X-ray Technician's face that told me what I wasn't prepared to hear. Something wasn't right. Although she never uttered a word, my spirit bore witness just the same. "Okay," she said in an upbeat voice, trying to conceal her true feelings. "The results will be sent to your doctor and he'll discuss them with you." She never gave eye contact. At least look at me, I thought, feeling ostracized.

"She," I said aloud as I hurriedly redressed.
"Excuse me, "she said, puzzled.
"You said, he," I retorted. "My doctor is a she. She will contact me with the results."

The technician turned away, not willing to engage me. I quickly exited the examination room. I must admit that was the longest walk down the hall, out the door to my car. As I glanced at my female-comrades, waiting, anticipating better results. I silently prayed for the same.

Days turned into weeks, still no word from my doctor. Maybe it was a false alarm, I supposed. So I waited like a good patient, still nothing. I eventually called to inquire about my test results. The office assistant seemed annoyed that I called, but read the results to me over the phone anyway.

"Oh, you need a sonogram," she said nonchalantly. "There were concerns with your mammogram."

I was listening but didn't hear her. "And when were you going to tell me?" I asked, upset.

"Uh, it's the patient's responsibility to call us regarding their results, not ours," she defended.

Years later, I ended up returning to that same Dr.'s office for a minor medical need. Browsing my record, my doctor asked why I haven't been there in several years. I told her. She was disappointed, wishing I had reported the incident instead of not returning.

In retrospect, maybe I should have informed the doctor of the occurrence. I just didn't have time for the negative energy in or around my life at the time. I knew those next few days would be a test of faith. I told no one. I didn't want to deal with the possible jagged faith of my love circle, while having to deal with my pending situation. It was too much.

I imagined myself, as I'd often do when under imminent fear, wrapped in the bosom of Jesus, protected by God Himself and the heavenly host. And there I stayed, night and day, in love and peace knowing I was healed and whole from my head to my toes. This was my truth and I was sticking to it!

During the sonogram, I was nervous but held close to my faith. This wasn't my first rodeo. I have been tried and tested and knew the blood of Jesus was sufficient enough to heal, repair, or restore my body like before. And as long as God was there, I was in the best care.

The doctor was thorough. As she pressed deeper to get a closer look, my body began to tremble. What the hell? I thought grimacing. "Gently, gently." I silently instructed. Suddenly one of my maternal grandmother's sayings came to mind, "Whatever you have to go through in life, do it in Jesus' name. Lean on Him when you can't stand on your own." I did just that. Continually thanking Him for a favorable report.

Diagnosis: Fibrocystic breast- noncancerous breast lumps affecting over half the women population. Thank God, I sighed in relief.

14.
Just as I am

Do you love me, accept me just as I am? Better yet, do I love myself, honor myself as I am? The proof is in my truth - what I do and allow others to do.

F

Take me just as I am or leave me alone. Don't try to change me, only God can do that. I'm over half a century now, so just let me be me. I know right from wrong. I've read the whole entire Bible at least 4 times. I know I'm a great person with a fun, humorous personality. I would like to be a housewife instead of going to a 9 to 5.

A man can work from dusk till dawn, but a woman's work is never done (Jean Little, Orphan at My Door: The Home Child Diary of Victoria Cope). I am who God ordained me to be before I was even formed in my mother's womb (Jeremiah 1:5). I am alive. I am loved. I am blessed. I am favored. I am grateful. I am forgiving.

I am healed. I am whole. I am courageous. I am victorious. I am determined. I am gifted. I am anointed. I am confident. I am successful. I am unstoppable. I am generous. I am joyous. I am beautiful. I am God's masterpiece.

Be yourself. Don't try to imitate others. Jehovah made us all unique from His original format (Genesis 1: 27).

K

The proof is in the way we treat ourselves and allow others to treat us. Acceptance is acknowledgement. Only you can change yourself for the betterment of you. Whose blueprint of perfection are you following anyway?

I am a whole woman, having lived a few decades. With every life encounter, it sharpened me for the better. I realized early on that I was 50% my mother and 50% my father. Whatever that morphed me into, so be it. I am comfortable in my own skin.

People have told me my whole life different aspects of my physicality that needed improvement. When I was younger, some would say my skin was a nice tone, but my nose was too prominent. I breathe just fine so I never saw a need to alter it.

Others have said I had a pretty face, but my natural hair didn't work for me. Rather, it didn't work for them. Most of them had relaxed hair which didn't seemingly give them an advantage in any way. So however my hair grew in its natural state has always been alright with me.

I've always been satisfied with the way I am and felt I was well-made (Psalm 139:14), even with areas I thought needed enhancement. Thank you, Lord, for making me perfect in Your image!

I have also been called cold and heartless. I think not. I have the right not to intertwine my life with mess and foolishness. If that makes me mean, oh well. I call it self-care.

We create the lives that we want by choice or default; either way, we are the creators. Being passive doesn't give us a pass in life either. It just means we were silent participants. So it's only fair that we deal with our creations. And just like we created, we can recreate our life to support our desired lifestyle, not only for ourselves but for the betterment of generations to come.

We can't pick and choose after we've made a mess of things. I have to deal with my choices, positive or negative. You must deal with yours. A misconception of many is, not only do we deal with ours, but theirs too. It's said to be the Christian thing to do. The hell you preach! It's enough bearing my own cross, let alone having to bear others. I have no problem helping those who want to help themselves. But for those who want nothing and do nothing, the answer is no.

I have witnessed firsthand, and I'm sure you too, others cruising through life with no intention of driving themselves. They lean and cling to you for everything until you are depleted. Then off they go to whomever or whatever won't tell them no. I call them love-suckers. They are like parasites, depleting your love-well until it's dry. Why? They know you love and care about them which is a manipulative play on your emotions. They take and take, never giving in return. It obviously works. They keep doing and you keep giving.

It took me some time but I eventually got there. I had to learn to love them at a distance for my own happiness and peace of mind. I will always hope for the best for them. But reality dictates, like Iyanla Vanzant, that I "call a thing a thing!" They are doing what works for them and I must do the same. I choose to love myself up, not down to their level.

So, when life is chastising or correcting someone, we should not interfere with universal order. Either they are going to get the lesson or not. But whatever their consequences are, they aren't ours to bear. Have you noticed that every time we get out of our lane to intervene, our life ends up wrecked in some way?

I'm reminded of what a former supervisor, Kathy, would often say. "Behavior is a choice." I have always been a fixer, trying to save the world. Repeated knocks across the head finally got my attention. I was out of line and out of order. People who don't want to be fixed, won't, no matter our time or efforts.

I realized that change comes from the inside out, rather than the outside in. You can inundate a person with support and services and their life will be none the better, the next day or decades later. Look at our welfare system and like organizations. Resources and staff are overwhelmed, exhausted. I believe that only when we change the heart, will the mind and body follow.

Love yourself just as you are. If you want to perfect an area, so be it. But if you are changing or altering your DNA in any way, seek counseling. There is something inside that's affecting your outer perception. I find it hard enough to be me, let alone trying to be someone else. I don't need celebrity validation. I am my own role model and I alone hold that honor. Can't anyone do me quite like me. That's why I love myself just as I am.

15.
Keepsake

Your most prized possession is your cherished keepsake. What is yours? Wherever you spend most your time, money, or put the highest value (in thought, action or energy) is where your heart is.

F

A keepsake to me is having true relationships that stand the test of time. I had a cherished relationship once – my failed marriage. All the early signs said, no. But my heart said, yes. He was still legally married when we started dating, which was wrong. Even though he and his wife were separated, I should not have dated a married man. In short, he cheated on me, like he cheated on her and all the other "hers" in his life.

The year was 2000. I was having a 70's party and I wanted him to come. I went looking for him at his old apartment, but he had moved. When our eyes finally met sometime later, it was like, "Where have you been all these years?" We enjoyed spending time with one another during this encounter. Although he was a little intoxicated, we still had a good time. His drinking would prove to be detrimental to our marriage in the long run.

Before we started dating, I asked him if he was still married. He said, "Yes, but we're separated." Right then and there, I should have gone about my own business. But I didn't. I stayed and eventually paid the ultimate price.

At the beginning of our courtship, we immediately started discussing marriage. I told him I wanted a boy and a girl, and to be a housewife. He said he had children already and didn't want anymore. I responded, "You have them, but I don't." He countered, "Well, okay. We can have a boy, since I didn't get a chance to raise my son." He also said, "You can be a housewife, because I make enough money."

We had a long-distance relationship for a year and a half. When I visited him in San Antonio, different females would call his apartment all the time, but never his wife. While dating, he bought me a Ford Mustang. My mom wanted to know why he was buying me a car and wasn't divorced. He told her that he bought me the car because he wanted me to look stylish. I guess he was ashamed of my Ford Escort. He also told her he wasn't divorced because his wife would not give him one. My sister remedied that by drafting the divorce papers for him, and that was a done deal.

One day, he came to my house and told my mother that I didn't want to work. He couldn't understand that as I had a college degree. So after he complained to her about me, she felt as if his antics reminded her of her ex-husband and questioned whether I should marry him. I told her that I was certain. My time clock was running out for having babies, and that he really loved me.

I loved that man. He was so good to me. He was tall, dark, somewhat handsome, muscular, sweet and funny. However, his downfall was that he drank too much. Nonetheless, he had a great job and was a great provider.

As I mentioned before, he bought me a car, gave me money, got me a lot of gifts for Christmas and always told me that he loved me. He reassured me time and time again that he was a changed man. I believed him, so we got married in 2002 and eventually had 2 beautiful children, a boy and a girl. Our life together was marvelous, until I got pregnant with my daughter. When I told him I was pregnant, he looked at me and said, "I didn't want another baby with you!" My heart dropped.

I later found out that he had another daughter that I was unaware of. I was tricked because I told him from the beginning, that I didn't want to marry a man with more than 2 children. At that point, it was too late, because I was madly in love.

The whole time I was pregnant with our daughter, he cheated on me. After she was born, he went 2 months without talking to me. This was so he could go and come as he please without having to give an explanation. He would go pick up his other children without me. And, even take them places and not invite me.

My ex-husband asked for a divorce on my birthday. He filed for divorce on our 7th anniversary. I guess he chose days that were memorable events; days that would stay etched in my mind so that I'd never forget. He brought his lover into our home, as if she was a friend. This friend is now his current wife. He was physically, mentally, and emotionally abusive. My ex actually lived the single life the entire time we were married. He treated me just like he treated his first wife. Yes, I reaped what I sowed (Galatians 6:7-9) for dating a married man. My ex, the deacon, was definitely a womanizer.

Today, I don't have any ill feelings towards him, and I'm not a scorned woman. Why? Because, I'm a child of the King. I know God has someone who will love me, for me. And if you are divorced, start thanking God in advance for your mate, now. You deserve to be happy, loved and valued.

K

Sorry if you fall a far second, third, or forth on the keepsake scale. If you love anything more than you love yourself, you need to re-evaluate your priorities. You are the most precious, valuable of anything. Never love anyone or anything more than you love yourself. There's only one of you. Keep yourself safe.

I would say the one thing I cherish more than anything would be life. To say that tomorrow is not promised would be just cliché. I have had so many losses in my life. I'm surprised that I'm still standing. I know this may sound awful but I have solace in knowing that others have had it worse than me. It keeps me humbled, counting my blessings every day.

My earliest recollection of what I've learned to cherish most was when I was twelve years old. I watched my grandmother burn to death in a house fire. It was a warm summer night in late August, just past midnight in Kentucky. I was awakened by a nudge by an unseen energy that whispered subliminally, "Wake-up. It's time." Perhaps it was the voice of an angel, I'm not sure. However, days prior, the same intuitive voice asked me what I'd do if my grandmother's house caught on fire. Ironically, now that I think back on it, she was not in my twelve year old escape plan. My heart now cries at this almost forty year old revelation.

I responded to the angel's question with unwaveringness, "I'd take Rob and Angie into the bathroom, shut the door behind us, turn the basin and tub faucets on to allow water to escape out the drains, while the three of us submerged ourselves down in the tub. I'd also open the window about an inch high so that any smoke that entered the bathroom would escape over our heads and out the ajar window."

The voice responded, "You answered wisely."

The night of the house fire, my sister, Angie wasn't able to spend the night. So, it was just my grandmother, Mary Evelyn, my brother, Rob and I there. Mama, who we affectionately called our paternal grandmother, had just gotten out of the hospital. Still weak, she tried to light a cigarette and the rest was history.

Oddly, the Fire Department was located on the next block just down the street. The house phone had melted on the wall. But for some strange reason, I was still able to call my dad's house. My stepmother answered. I told her that the house was on fire.

When the First Responders arrived, they were quick into action. I recall being dazed, feeling numb. Rob and I were exhausted, having done all we knew to do to save Mama, to no avail. The grown-ups were in control, finally. Our faith was in their hands. Surely, they would fix it and make it right. Mama was our life.

Ms. Ruth, an elderly neighbor across the street, had asked the neighborhood children earlier that summer not to make a lot of noise at night because it disturbed her ailing father who was bed-ridden. Of course, Rob, Angie and I obeyed; the other children in the neighborhood, not so much.

Within less than an hour, which seemed like an eternity, out of my peripheral vision, I saw the firemen bring what was left of my grandmother's remains out in a black bag. Still, the finality didn't register with me right then. I believe I was more in awe at the volume of sight-seekers aligning the curb, flashing police lights, ambulance and fire trunks. It looked like a scene from a motion picture, just before the credits rolled.

Ms. Ruth walked across the street straight towards me. Surely she wasn't approaching me to fuss. The noise was coming from the first responders, not Robbie and me, I was ready to defend. We already felt like slaughtered lambs. We just couldn't take being fussed at, now.

Before I knew it, Ms. Ruth scooped me into her arms like a newborn baby. How she was able to hold a twelve year old, at her age, was baffling. I returned the loving embrace. It was uncommon to get affection from adults in that era so I basked in the moment. My soul began to rest. I needed a touch, caress from somebody, anybody. I wanted my mom who was in Louisiana. She wasn't there so Ms. Ruth had to stand in her stead. Ms. Ruth whispered, "It's going' to be okay, baby," as she gently patted my back. "Go 'head. Let it out!"

With her permission, I howled from the innermost depths of my being. You could hear my fervent cry for miles. Rob joined in concert. He was a shy boy that rarely had much to say, got in trouble, or spanked for that matter. But this unfortunate incident warranted our emotions to be unleashed. And when the flood gates opened, the tsunami roared, not only that night, but many grief-stricken nights to come, changing who Rob and I were and who we'd forever become.

A few years later, my sister Angie, now sixteen was beaten to death by her boyfriend, killing her, and her unborn baby. She missed death by fire in 1976. But fate caught up with her in 1983 just the same. I was eighteen years old when my sister was slain.

After my grandmother's death, I became nervous, shy, and less expressive, often stumbling over words; unable to connect thoughts, let alone sentences or phrases. My ability to hear was also affected. I could hear a person talking, but not necessarily understand what they were saying or if they were even talking to me. Their voices were like background noises. After being popped a couple of times by my mother for ignoring her, I learned quickly to improvise. I'd pause, listen attentively and often turn towards the person as if my whole being tried to fill in where my hearing could not.

After Angie was murdered, I was certain that the heavens didn't like me for some strange reason. I felt cursed. I was shell-shocked- afraid to love or be loved, for fear that anything I loved would leave me grief-stricken and alone. The hole in my soul ran deep. It hurt too much to love and lose. So at eighteen, I began to love at a distance, starting with my new college BFF Felicia. Relationships felt safer this way, more manageable. We were both impressionable and naïve, so my distancing was checked off as my being aloof or a loner, which still somewhat exists today.

So, my keepsake is life. It is the most precious gift I have been given. For I realize that regardless of the trials and tribulations I've had to and still endure, I'm still here. The old saying reigns true, "What doesn't kill you, makes you stronger." It may take you some time to get to this resolve, but you will. Just know that life is a continuum of lessons, one success, mistake, or disappointment at a time. I wouldn't exchange any part of this journey I'm on now. It has made me stronger, wiser, more empathetic, forgiving and loving.

Because of my experiences, I no longer flip or trip over miniscule things. They seem so insignificant in comparison to what I've lived through. You get to this place of acceptance and appreciation by accumulating experience and achieving maturity. And, I have the emotional battle scars to prove it. Notice I didn't say wounds, because a wound is a sore that hasn't healed.

If you are still carrying around old wounds of past hurt, pain, or injustice, you haven't healed or moved on. You will never live in your now if you stay in what was or what has been.

16.
Heartbreak

Sometimes the only way to have a healthy heart is for it to be broken so it can mend properly. Stop holding on to situations that give you heart palpitations. Face the truth. Your heart is out of rhythm because you and that person are out of sync.

F

A broken heart is something only Jesus Christ, our Lord and Savior can fix. Oh, and also time. Time heals all wounds (Psalm 147:3). My very first broken heart I can remember was when my mom and dad separated. I was around nine years old at the time. We were riding in the car with my dad and he said, "Kids I have something to tell you!" We said, "What?" He replied, "Your mom and I are getting separated." I said, "What that mean?" He explained, "It means we will not be living together anymore." I exclaimed, "No way. I don't believe that!" And true enough, it happened. They moved apart, and eventually divorced. However, he did still stay in our lives. For my parents to divorce was terribly heart breaking for me.

My dad taught me many important life lessons over the years to limit future heartbreaks. But I experienced them anyway. I remember when I was in high school my dad told me that I was beautiful, intelligent, and fine. He did this in efforts to raise my self-esteem in case boys tried to lower it. Because my worth was already implanted by my dad, no boy could uproot it.

My heart would also break every time someone close to me died or when I'd disappoint Jesus. Every time I sin intentionally, I'd feel just awful. It's like, I knew better, and I should obey the Ten Commandments, but my flesh would sometimes get weak, or temptation gets the best of me. I'd often pray that God would forgive me, and I'd try not to repeat my sinful ways. Unfortunately, I'd end up sinning still. I'm so glad that Jesus paid the price for my justification. I love the Lord. He heard my cry (Psalm 34:17).

When I wanted to marry a guy, but he didn't choose me, or vice versa, this would oftentimes break my heart as well. I believe my biggest and most overwhelming heartbreak was when I had to leave my six year old daughter and eight year old son in San Antonio, TX with their father and his third wife, his mistress. After my unfair divorce, I stayed in Texas two years fighting for my children. Then, I heard about a couple who fought over their son until he was grown, just throwing money away! Two years was enough for me.

My ex-husband didn't want to pay child support to me because he was still paying it to his first wife. So I reluctantly agreed to let him keep our children during the school year in San Antonio. I felt that Texas schools were better than Louisiana's. It ended up working out perfectly. I'd keep our children during the summer months and holidays.

When I first got back home to Louisiana, I missed my babies so much that I was having anxiety attacks. As time went on, I got used to my freedom. I psyched myself out by saying, "No more homework, no more school meetings, no more schedules. I'll have them during vacation time. We'd get to enjoy the fun times like, swimming, roller skating, church, Chuck-E-Cheese, birthday parties, etc." And so we did and continue to do so.

K

Things don't work out for a reason. If you never end one chapter, how will you start a new one? It may sound like an oxymoron but I believe when things go awry, it's a golden opportunity for things to go right.

If life was always peaches and cream, as it is for some, when things go left or a tragedy occurs, they fall apart, even to the point of suicide. I can't count the times my heart has been broken so I'll lump all the feelings into one. Heartbreak hurts like hell. Sometimes it's all you can do to pick yourself up off the floor. Each heartbreak mended me into a work of art, a masterpiece piece, entitled woman; and a better one at that.

If you become bitter, hateful or revengeful, you stay in that space and emit negative energy to every subsequent relationship. Had many break-ups? Tell the truth and shame the devil (Shakespeare, William, Henry IV. Part I, 1597). Maybe it's not them. Perhaps, it's you. If you stay stuck, you can't move or grow. Just look at people you know that are still whining about the past, justifying their reasons for holding on to the pain or misery.

When I look back over situations and honestly reflect, I realize that I am much better off without them than I'd be with them. Whatever part of you that's holding to yesterday is preventing your today. It is imperative that you **feel** the hurt. Stop pretending that it didn't wound you. We try to null our pain, guilt, or shame with food, depression or expensive toys (human and inanimate), etcetera.

Deal with the hurt. It was what it was. Now that it's no more, what did the experience teach you? Did you learn anything? Remember what we fail to heed, we often repeat.

Heal the hurt. Check it off as a life lesson learned. Be strong and move on. Seek professional intervention, if need be. There is no shame in getting counseling. Take care of yourself by any means necessary. You are not Superman or Superwoman. They aren't real and don't deal with real life issues. But, you do.

Begin blueprinting your heart and mind the way you'd want true love, happiness, and prosperity to look and feel like right now, in this present moment. See yourself happy, loving yourself in every drawing/pen stroke of this new life you are creating. Some of us struggle to simply see past the pain. But in order for us to move forward, we have to gain new insight in order to change our life paths. If not, we're sure to repeat the same old life script.

Love is a beautiful emotion. It keeps you in a state of bliss. But in order to realize its fullness, you have to experience its opposite, pain. **F**eel, **D**eal and **H**eal! So, whenever you experience a heartbreak, take it in stride. Choose to live, not die. Get back on life's horse and ride, baby ride!

17.
Connection

Be mindful of your connectivity- the socket you plug into. It only takes one to energize you. If you have a dependency on multiple outlets to get a jolt, maybe it isn't the socket, it's you.

F

The best connection to have in this life is with Jesus Christ, our Lord. If you are connected to our Savior with all your heart, soul, and mind, your life will be fulfilling. If you are connected to or associated with the wrong type of people, then you will be headed down the road to a life of heartache and pain.

Sometimes we socialize with bad company because we grew up with them, or we feel obligated to them for one reason, or another. We often times hang with these people, thinking we can change them, but in reality, they are slowly changing us. One may say, "If you go to church with me, I'll go to the club with you." Remember, birds of a feather flock together (William Turner, 1545 The Rescuing of Romish Fox).

When you continue to hang around people who mean you no good, you will regret it sooner, if not later. Your reputation will be ruined. You will not be trusted by neither family nor friends. You might lose your career or get into trouble that costs you thousands. Or worse, end up in jail, or possibly six feet under.

If you don't want a disastrous life, hang around God-fearing, positive, non-jealous, loving, kind-hearted people. Matthew 6:24 states, "No one can serve two masters. Either you will hate the one, and love the other, or you will be devoted to the one and despise the other. You cannot serve both God and money."

K

An appetite, like a habit, starts with one bite at a time. We create the over- indulgence and then wonder why we are never satisfied. With that being said, let me digress to another kind of connection. The type of connection you keep; one of a spiritual nature between you and your pastor, priest or rabbi. It can also be between you and a trusted friend, neighbor, or even a stranger.

The connectivity is the same just as long as the two of you are connected by the Heart of the Living God. Note I made a point of emphasizing the Living God because a lot of people, churches, and temples don't really believe in God. If they did, the world would not be in the state it's in today and we couldn't treat our fellowman anyway. I'm just saying.

January 25, 2015, around 4:00 a.m., I received a call from the hospital. I was in a daze from my interrupted sleep as the doctor asked my permission, being the next of kin, to perform emergency surgery on my mother as she was hemorrhaging to death. I had just spoken to her hours earlier and she sounded okay, being her same old jovial self. So the doctor's comment took me by surprise. I consented with sadness.

While my immediate family slept, I was on the highway in route to Shreveport. Even though I've driven this trip a thousand times before, I ended up taking a different route. Instead of Highway 80 to I-20, I took 635 East to I-20, which added additional miles to my trip. Now that I look back on it, it was divine intervention. I needed that quiet time with God. The eastern sunrise from I-20 was breathtaking, surreal. I wasn't prepared to lose my mom. But I guess no one ever is.

Although I left alone, I wasn't alone. I could sense my spiritual crew riding along beside me. I needed them and they showed up strong. You can't tell me that God and the heavenly hosts aren't real because their presence I felt in that car with me. I knew my mom was going to pull through, even if all signs said otherwise. I just chose to believe the report of the Lord (Isaiah 53:1).

As the sun rose on that drive to Shreveport, I metaphorically saw it as God rising in the operating room, restoring my mother's health better than before. That became my belief and I was sticking to it! After weeks of ICU and rehabilitative care, I am immensely grateful that my mom is still in the land of the living. My heart goes out to others who don't have that same report. My prayer is that God will soothe their hearts and give them peace.

The connection I would like to expound upon, is the relationship with the man or woman of your house of worship, known respectfully as bishops, pastors, priests, rabbis, etc. My Bishop has always been there for my family over the years, through deaths, births, disappointments and celebrations. With my mom's unexpected illness, his mission remained the same, always a phone call or hospital visit away.

During this last scare with my mother, Bishop Brite and the New Testament Church family came through in a big way. For that, I will always be eternally grateful to him and the saints of God, near and far. Little did we know at the time, that he himself was ill and needed hospitalization.

I hear people brag about their mega churches and mega pastors as though that means anything. Does your mega pastor know you by name? In times of crisis, do you have your mega pastor's number on speed dial? Will your mega pastor come to your aid? I rest my case.

Some may see my home church as having antiquated beliefs. Differences of opinions, we all have them. It doesn't mean that one's right and the other's wrong. I consider myself to be spiritual, not religious, so I don't subscribe to old school religious dogma anyway. But when it comes down to what's important, the things of God, I'm all in.

When we diminish God to what a person wears, dancing, or drinking sociably, we have missed the bigger picture- love, beyond judgment. I am blessed to have a connection to a church, even with old fashion beliefs, can still get a prayer through. This is the connection you keep, regardless of secular variances. When you need them, they are there.

Life has taught me that religious, political, or racial differences mean nothing when you or your loved ones need intervention and need it now! So I give permission to whomever, whatever church you attend, or beliefs you may have, to pray for me. I need your connection. I am a living witness that prayer changes things.

18.
Journey

Journeys take you to places unchartered, giving you memories and experiences of a lifetime. Remember where you've been. Know where you're going.

F

My life's journey has been an excellent one. I was the second child born to my parents, Lorenza Bell, Jr. and Maxine Moch. They were terrific parents in my eyes. They didn't curse or smoke. And they provided a loving, caring home for my sister, brother and me. After they divorced, my dad made it a point to still be in our lives. I was around eight years young at the time.

I never like school much, but I graduated high school and college with honors. College was a great learning experience. After college, I went to Manicuring School. Anyone need a manicure or pedicure? While doing nails, I became a substitute teacher, as well as holding many other jobs.

I always wanted to land a national commercial. I'm still working on that dream. In the beginning, I had a great marriage. From that union, we had two wonderful children: my boy first, then 19 and ¾ months later, my daughter. Yes, God blessed me with my pride and joy. We had the storybook family, until my ex-husband started creeping. He divorced me and made my life even better. God kept me, and I'm enjoying life to the fullest.

My journey has been one I can't complain about, and I love it.... the good, with the not so good.

K

You can run here and there for peace and happiness. But the one place you can never journey from is yourself. Learn to find peace within and enjoy being your own best friend. We can all agree that life is a journey. We stay the course until we've reached our final destination. My take on journey is discovering one of the most undiscovered locations there is, you.

I know a lot of people who do not like their own company, being by themselves. They just got to have a man/woman or friends/family around at all times. They would rather be anywhere, with anyone, doing anything rather than being alone.

We are all walking transcripts or resumes; our past telling a lot about our present and future. We try to conceal our truth by being the life of the party, wanting to be seen and admired. Not to mention our banners of success, from cars, houses, to body ornaments we wear proudly on our sleeves, pleading, "See me, please!"

We see you, but don't care. That's your financial or emotional debt to bear, especially if it's for the wrong reasons like a person's looks or how they cook in the kitchen- hint, hint! On this journey in our lives, we should know who we are, what we want and where we are going, even if we have to do it solo. We can journey the world over, but until we discover who we really are and our true purpose on earth, we're just wandering aimlessly.

Get to know yourself. Do the things you like to do, even if you have to do it alone. This is how you discover who you really are and what you are truly made of. You will be in a position to meet new acquaintances and experience new things.

Take chances. Accept new challenges. Head out on new adventures. Leave family and friends. They'll be okay until you return. Don't feel you have to travel the globe. Your discovery could be right there in your own home and community.

You can't be all things to everyone else, neglecting what's most important- yourself. Start with a manicure and pedicure. Get a new hair-dew by a different hair stylist who doesn't know you. Take a trip to the book store, grab a cappuccino and read a book or magazine of interest. Let your imagination take you to undiscovered destinations.

Look at the personal possessions you've collected over the years. Start with yourself, those few extra pounds. Map out a plan of action of cleaning your temple (body) as you de-clutter your castle (home). Once you've become reacquainted with you and yours, you won't have a problem enjoying new discoveries in and around you. And when you take the joy of you on another excursion, you will realize that you are the journey, not the destination. And wherever you are, there is love, peace, joy and happiness.

19.
Cha-Ching

Getting paid for your trade!
What's your worth, value?

F

Cha-Ching! Cha-Ching! Yes, money is what makes the world go round. Without it, you pretty much won't have anything. That's why we have to work, which is part of God's plan for our lives. The man who doesn't work….doesn't eat (II Thessalonians 3:10). Since God made the man the head of his household and the woman his help-mate, this means that someone has to work until their brow sweats.

It's amazing what people will do for the mighty dollar. Some have sold their souls for it. When some people see money, their eyes get big. If you find money on the ground, you get excited. Winning money at the casino is a rush, until you play it all back, lose your money and the extra you won. There are many ways to receive money. However you gain your increase, 10% belongs to the Lord along with offerings. Don't ever let money get the best of you. Save for a rainy day. Leave an inheritance for your children and grandchildren (Proverbs 13:22). Remember, the love of money is the root to all evil (I Timothy 6:10).

K

Never become complacent with where you are. You may have to challenge yourself to grow. The same mundane job will make you insane. So if you stay, you really are crazy! The school of life is always open to teach so you can reach your full potential. Move with knowledge and technology for your own psychology. Learn something new every day. And while you are learning, get paid for your trade!

At a quarterly table-topics event at Fern's, Denise made a comment that I found insightful. She said, "Being paid your worth." Although I've heard this statement countless times before, this time, it resonated in my spirit. I felt it.

I've always been laid back and allowing, never challenging status quo, whatever was whatever. Like the Apostle Paul, I had learned to be contented (Philippians 4:11). But a change had come over me. And Denise's statement, along with being around friends who were movers and shakers in their respective fields, had ignited a fire inside me that wouldn't be quenched. I was working a fulltime job. However, I was not being paid my worth.

Why not me? I constantly mused. I was just as intelligent and capable as others. I just needed the opportunity. And if employers weren't going to give it to me, I had to make it happen myself. Most of my professional career has been working in state jobs. People either retired or died in their positions, making advancement literally impossible.

I have always enjoyed serving others regardless of the pay. It didn't take me long to realize that there was no real value in being overworked and underpaid, not to mention the feeling of being undervalued; all of which was a mindset. So I changed my mind. I had a new life mission and I was in it to win it!

Like everyone else, I liked nice things and had a family to support. Jesus hadn't given me a million dollars yet, no matter how often The Church would tell me to "just believe." And like a good Christian, I waited on Jesus to fix it, deliver me. It hardly rained in Texas so I didn't expect money to fall from the sky anytime soon. After a lifetime of waiting, it finally dawned on me, that perhaps Jesus was waiting on me.

"You ain't no punk and you don't serve a punk God!" Infamous words of Pastor Isiah Joshua, Jr. kept resurfacing. Out of the many messages he's preached, this one standing out. Now one of my main mantras, I keep it at the forefront of every thought, every action.

So, what I had an Associate's, Bachelor's, and Master's degree? The reality was people with no degrees were making more money than me. Good for them, not so good for me. I reminded myself again of who I was and whose I was. And that the source of my resource was within me.

We determine our worth, not a job, or a company. So with the writing of this book, my and Felicia's retirement plan (Laugh), I have shifted my thinking to a billionaire's mindset. Think you can't? I know you can because you are no punk and you don't serve a punk God! Join us at the top! Cha-Ching!

20.
The Ties That Bind

We have relationships to fulfill our human need to be connected. It's natural and needed. However, some connections should be broken or distanced for our own self-care and well-being.

F

The tie that binds will meet us always. Therefore, I must make sure I am binding with the right ties. When you are connected to someone who uplifts and encourages you, that's a good thing. But if you are engaged in evil, get ready to suffer the consequences. I have two ties I am bound to: my son, Ray Jr. and my lovely daughter, Fee-Fee. Now the love I have for my children cannot, and will not, be broken.

The glue that binds my family together is the blood of Jesus. There is power in the blood (Hebrews 9:22). Without faith, all ties will be destroyed. The ties that bind us to Christ are our love, faith, hope, prayers, trust, obedience, sincerity, humbleness, honesty, repentance, forgiveness, belief, acceptance, confession, righteousness, and the fear of God.

My ex-husband was bound to me until he broke God's covenant. When you go creeping outside of your marriage, the ties you had with your spouse will be torn down. To keep your ties binding, stay faithful to one another and don't go outside of your marriage, committing extra-marital affairs.

K

You know who they are. They are the relationships that you can't distinguish between family, friend, or foe. And if it weren't for their perceived value in your life, you wouldn't share the same air-space with them. Intuitively you know they don't support your common good, yet you feel compelled to stay close, when all signs say stay away.

We are all intimately connected whether we believe it. I need you. You need me. Together, we can make or break a situation when we join forces; either for good or evil. What will our legacy be? Are we even capable of coming together for the greater good of humanity, not just for ourselves, but our children and children's children?

We see firsthand the violence; turmoil religious and political differences can cause. What about family and friendship differences? Are we that naïve to believe that just because they are a relative or a friend that they really have our best interests at heart?

As I have previously mentioned, God has gifted each of us with an internal thermostat, an emotional gauge, a sense-feeling apparatus that tells us the truth. We know when we are happy, sad, or when we get that inkling that something just isn't right. We often shut it off when it comes to family and friends which is definitely a no-no. This is the time we really need to pay special attention because of our emotional attachment to our loved ones. Because of the closeness, we can sometimes get mixed messages, skewed vibes. We hope for the best, never wanting to see the obvious.

Be aware of the ties that you bind. Relative, close friend or not, if they don't support your success, bring you love, joy or peace, let them be. You are aware of how they make you feel. So what if they are your parents, siblings, best friends or mate? They are the ones who will hurt you the most because they are closest to you. People in the streets, you won't allow to get that close to you.

I have learned to take people at face value. They are who they are and do what they do. So I'm not shocked when they do something inappropriate. Yes, I hope for better. But people will not love or treat you better than they do themselves. So if they don't give a damn about what's theirs, don't be foolish enough to believe they care about what's yours. Oh you of ignorant faith!

If they are sneaky, conniving, low-down, and no-good, their place in your heart doesn't change who they are or what they are capable of. This has been the hardest lesson for me to learn. People only do to you what you allow them to do. If you wouldn't put up with it, they wouldn't do it, even family and friends.

Our problem is that we put up with it and expect a different outcome. Now who is the insane one? Break ties that don't support your success. Love them at a distance if you have to, but don't be anyone's fool.

Establish new ties with people who inspire and substantiate you. It's love, not blood that binds. And love is synonymous with trust and respect. You can't have one without the other.

If you are the sharpest and smartest in your circle, expand your net a little further. You can't grow from what you already know. Character and integrity go a long way and are kindred. If either is ever in question, that's the life lesson. You don't have to wonder, life has just schooled you. Pass the test and move on.

21.
Revolving Door

Sometimes life can seem like a revolving door. In and out, the same mundane route; the similar, familiar.

F

Revolving Door to me means repeating things. The same ole, same ole! Just can't seem to get it together. You try, but it's almost like déjà vu. Here I go again. Why do I keep making the same mistakes over and over?

Examples of a revolving door to me are the following: people who are in and out of jail all the time, children who are in and out of their parent's home, Christians who go to church on and off, citizens who go from job to job, single women with children who move from house to apartment, males who have multiple females in their lives. In my case, I would say my revolving door is dating. I meet different men, but they turn out to be cheap, too short, not built enough, too young, controlling, too old, or married. Did I say cheap, too?

K

Let's not pretend. We are the reasons why we are in the mess we're in. Remember lessons we fail to heed, repeat. I had to learn late in life that people are the way they are and the knowledge of this truth was the universe's way of teaching me. To expect anything more, would be to deny universal fact.

Like many of you, I'm sure you've given the benefit of doubt, hoping for better results, only to experience time and time again, disappointment and heartbreak. Yet, you hold out for hope anyhow, realizing if there is breath in their bodies, they still can change their life path. And my one desire for anyone that crosses my path, is the best life they can possibly muster. If I can do anything, in reason, to affect that possibility, I'm willing to do it.

I have loaned money, rather let money go, never seeing a cent of it returned. What's ironic is that they have the audacity to ask for more and display an attitude if I question or remind them of their indebtedness, or just say, no.

I have also intervened in situations when I should've allowed life to kick them in their asses. It's that hope thing again. Hoping for the best, but getting more foolishness instead.

Like many times before, they become irate if I tell them of their ways. They would say, "How dare you with your uppity, self-righteous self?" Really? I'd think in disbelief. Yet, they want money from my uppity, self-righteous, worked for myself, self (Laugh)! What's wrong with that picture?

A revolving door mentality will take all you have because it's non-stop. People who aren't responsible, stay irresponsible. Your intervention won't change a thing. If it did, they wouldn't return again and again.

Whatever life lesson they need to learn, let them learn it without you. If experience is the best teacher, let it do its job! If not, your relationship with them will be strained to the point that you'll hate to see them coming, and will try to avoid them altogether.

Just like there are love-suckers that take your love for granted, there are money-suckers that will take your money for granted too. Teach them money management if you really want to help them. Of course, they don't want to hear how to better manage their money, they just want to spend yours free and clear.

Like anything in life, if you abuse it, you lose it. So don't be a revolving door, enabling people to live beneath their best. Help them by helping them help themselves. Be a revolving door, no more!

22.

Oh, Hell to the NO!

Everyone has their own constitution that they live by; things they just WILL NOT accept or tolerate; the absolute deal breakers.

F

I will never ever get a tattoo. Leviticus 19:28 states, "Do not cut your body for the dead, nor put tattoo marks on yourselves. I am the Lord." I feel if the Lord wanted writings and pictures all over our bodies, we would have been born like that. Aren't birth marks enough? I guess not, the way I see some people all tatted-up. Insane! The sad part is, if one of your family members needed blood right away, you may not be able to help them because of state blood donation policies.

If someone ever made a claim, after I'm deceased, that I committed suicide, know that it's a lie! I love life too much to take my own. God said to live life and more abundantly (John 10:10), and that's what I do. I have a joy inside of me that no man can take away. I may be down sometimes, but I know without a shadow of a doubt, joy comes in the morning (Psalm 30:5). I am too blessed to be stressed or depressed! I'll never let the devil steal my joy for even a moment.

K

Life is about choices. You choose, win or lose. Either way you have to live with the consequences. If you stay in any situation, regardless of the reason, you're saying it's okay. In essence, you own what you condone!

Life is always teaching so class is always in. It doesn't matter whether you learn from personal experience or by being a voyeur in someone else's life. What's important is that you learn.

Two incidents come to mind. One, when I was around eighteen years old. The other, when I was in my early thirties. These two particular incidents opened my eyes to how volatile relationships can be.

Like I mentioned before, my sister, Angela and her unborn son were murdered at the hands of her boyfriend. How it got to this point, I'll never know. Her funeral was officiated by this young, flamboyant and handsome preacher. He drove a red Mercedes convertible. Wow! I thought. For a southern girl, I was in hog-heaven. He offered to take me to dinner soon thereafter. It's sad, but I don't recall his name. Anyway, he picked me up at my dad's. My dad had to make a point to introduce himself, firmly shaking the pastor's hand. It was so embarrassing. I couldn't wait to leave Kentucky and return to Louisiana.

The pastor and I ate dinner at an expensive restaurant. The food was really rich for my palate, but I chowed down anyway. He wanted to take me swimming afterwards at a private pool. But I didn't bring a swimsuit. I never thought of swimming any other way. Stop judging (Laugh)! So he made a phone call using a cordless mobile phone. I had never seen such a thing, except in James Bond movies. This was the early eighties. And gadgets like that were futuristic.

He called the owner of the boutique, telling the color and exact size of the bikini he planned to pick up for me. I was impressed that he even knew my measurements. I was so excited to be wined and dined, I must've jabbered the evening away. Before going to the boutique, we took a stroll through a park. If this was supposed to be romantic, I wasn't feeling it because the area was pitched black and barley lit.

I went along with it. *Maybe this was what couples did nowadays*, I imagined. I continued being my normal self, walking ahead, chattering his ear off, when out of the blue I felt a tingle down my back. *What the hell?* I thought, turning around. If that was supposed to feel good, it didn't. It hurt like hell.

I could see an object in the pastor's hand that resembled a stick. He no longer looked angelic, but devilish. *What the hell have I gotten myself into?* I thought, searching for an exit but none in sight. *Clever of him*, I assessed. He had isolated me to the point that no one could hear or see me. *Kudos, ass-hole*, I thought, now angered.

But he didn't know who he was messing with. I was going to get the hell out of there one way or another. I promised my parents I'd finish college. I had three more years to go. And that was that!

He struck me repeatedly on my arms and back. I guess I didn't submit quickly enough. One of Madear's saying immediately came to mind, "When you get your head in a lion's mouth, ease it out!" So I ran up to him and embraced him tightly. "I'm sorry," I said in a fake whimper. "Did I say something wrong?" The beating stopped. He felt empowered, in control.

The psycho ass-ho had the audacity to hold my hand as we drove back to my dad's. I played the game just to make it home safely. He had plans for a second date. *The hell you preach,* I thought, smiling. That would never happen in this life or the next.

I never told my parents until this writing. Why? I know my parents. Either one of them would've gotten a murder charge that night. We just buried my sister and nephew. Not to mention, losing my paternal grandmother a few years prior in a house fire. My heart just couldn't bear losing my parents as well. I checked it off as a lesson well learned. The pastor should've been grateful also. That night I spared his life.

The second incident wasn't physical. The cable guy and I only dated a few days. My exit occurred when tell-tale signs of his behavior were shown early on in our courtship. He got agitated over something as simple as my not passing him the remote control on one occasion, and my not answering the phone timely on another.

Thus, he called me "a stinkin', fuckin', ho-bitch!" *That was random*, I thought, shocked, not seeing what warranted such a violent outburst of rage. I instantly recognized the jolt in my emotional thermostat. God was telling me to pay attention, be aware. And, that I did.

There was no need for me to rationalize. It didn't look, sound, or feel right so that was reason enough for me. I paid attention to my senses, especially my intuition. It wasn't my job to stay around to teach or rehabilitate him. He needed a therapist for that.

If he could lose it over something so insignificant that soon into the relationship, what would the future hold? I had no plans to stay around long enough to find out. That did it for me! I was out of there!

And yes, I have been in other situations, not necessarily just with dates, but with people in general, whose ways troubled my spirit, but I tried to be a good Christian and foolishly remain their friends anyway for one reason or another. Now that I'm older and wiser, I know better and do better. If you see or feel trouble, be gone on the double!

So, my advice to you is not to beat yourself up if you are ever in a risky situation. Sometimes we just get there. The most important thing is to get yourself to safety; out of the mess, stress, or foolishness pronto. Ain't no shame in playing the game of survival! You succumb until you can run! Even if that means you don't get the last word. Zip your lip! Shhh!

All Honey-Boos are cool during the early stages of dating. In my circumstances, they showed me in the beginning who they were and it was up to me to stay or walk away. I sprinted.

Stop playing God. You can't change anyone. And if you see any sign of anger, rage or meanness, don't walk away, run! If you are currently in an unhealthy relationship, leave with the quickness. Your life and the safety of your children or future children depend on it!

23.
Retribution

Paying a debt that's owed.

F

Retribution is doing something good to make up for something bad you did in life. Starting over from a remorseful past is an awesome thing to accomplish. It can seem like a difficult time in your life to have to start all over again from scratch. But, there is nothing like a fresh start. The devil will try to discourage you from doing the right thing. You have to recognize when he sticks his head in your business, you have to stomp it back down into the ground. Rebuke Satan and keep looking towards the hills from which cometh your help (Psalm 121:1).

If you just call on the great name of Jesus, He will help you conquer all your fears. Once you have started over, gotten back on the right foot and repaid your debt back to society, you will feel much better about yourself. And you will only want the best at all times for yourself and others. Keep your head up, be responsible and stay positive. Make the right choices and always keep the peace.

K

We seem to live in a sin-conscience world. Every deed done must have a consequence. When things don't work out, we often think it's retribution from a previous wrong or misdeed. How about, it's life and life just happens!

When I was sixteen, I conned my older brother, Rob out of switching vehicles with me. I took my mom's Buick that he was driving and gave him our stepdad's old pick-up truck. Three friends and I were headed home from a house party in Lakeside, when we were sideswiped by a drunk driver who had just left the nightclub at the intersection of Centenary and Stoner Drive.

That evening, the saying, "God protects babies and fools" reigns true. First of all, as a teenager, I had no business driving after 11:00 p.m., Louisiana law. But I wanted to be cool and hang out with friends. That night almost cost me and my friends our lives.

We left that accident without a scratch. The fire department had to pry the driver's door open to get me out. As I lay in the graveyard next to tombstones, I figured I'd be joining the dead shortly, as soon as my mother arrived.

“Get up!” A familiar voice later demanded. I did as I was told. It made no sense to try and explain. I was wrong, plain and simple. And I just felt awful. If the graveyard would have swallowed me up, it would’ve been just fine.

The next day, I just lay in bed not wanting to face the music, patiently awaiting my doom. Earlier, my Uncles Buck and Jerry had calmed my mother’s nerves. So at least I was still breathing; alive to see another day.

To my surprise, I didn’t get a beat down or a royal cursing out. Maybe in fact my life was worth more valuable than a car. Thankfully, my mom forgave me. It took me a while to forgive myself for the hardship I put my family in. I was so sorry. I swore I’d never drive again.

The next day, my stepdad gave me the keys to the truck to run an errand. I questioned his logic. But nervously did as I was told. The lesson I learned was that mistakes happen. Sometimes you can be in the right and other times in the wrong. Regardless, ask for forgiveness, forgive yourself, and move on. Don’t beat yourself up. Refuse to keep misery as company.

And if a person has wronged you in some form or fashion, and they ask for forgiveness, oblige them. Sometimes the pain, guilt, shame or embarrassment of the mistake, is retribution enough. Don’t add injury to an already wounded soul.

24.
Bought Sense

Bought Sense is sense you had to pay a hefty price to finally get life's lesson; paid in full with the price of your behind being kicked and whipped into understanding.

F

Do you need a quarter so you can go buy yourself some sense? Common sense is better than book sense, anytime. Bought sense is when someone tells you that you will suffer the consequences for doing wrong, and you refuse to believe them. Instead, you believe it won't happen to you. You are a know-it-all, and will end up paying the ultimate price.

You go out and do something you know you should not be doing, because you think you're not going to get caught. You'll eventually have to pay the piper. There are many different ways to pay. One is with cash, now you are out of money. Second, you could go to prison. Third, you could lose your family. Fourth, you will lose your loved ones' trust. Last but not least, you could lose your life. So, what makes sense to me is....think before you act. Know the consequences of your actions before you partake in them. That way, you will be ahead of the game.

K

It's something about the human ego that thinks it's the crème de la crème. We assume that we are so special it won't happen to us because we are the "it" factor. Life will show us however, in more ways than one, that there's a price to pay when we ignore its warnings. Bought sense is the life lesson that we'll never have to be taught again. We got the lesson loud and clear!

When I was in graduate school, I was paying a fellow classmate to spend a few nights a week with her because she lived just walking distance from the college we attended. I would sometimes ride to Grambling State University on the Greyhound bus or catch a ride with another commuting graduate student. Monies were tight and I didn't have a car at the time.

On one of my trips back home, my key no longer fit the lock. I tried and tried to no avail. It never dawned on me that the lock could've been changed. If so, why and why wasn't I informed? Maybe it had slipped my part-time roommate's mind or something. Well, it didn't. She had put me out unbeknownst to me.

I only had a few more weeks to go before the end of the semester and desperately needed a temporary place to stay. Thankfully, Katie, another graduate student, allowed me to reside with her and her little girl until the semester ended.

Fast forward several years, I was in the wedding of another graduate school friend. Several classmates who attended college with us during that time were present. It was a joy seeing everybody.

One classmate had driven from up north to be a part of the wedding festivities. Since graduate school, I knew she didn't care much for me by her attitude and disposition towards me. Like me, I'm sure you can sense when someone doesn't really like you. So I kept a safe distance. I was too old for the foolishness then and now. You can imagine how surprised I was, when out of the blue, she struck up a conversation with me. *What the hell*, I thought. I must admit I was a bit surprised and suspicious.

To make the long story short, she felt a need to let me know that she hated me during graduate school, thinking I was having an affair with her husband. *No shit*, I thought arrogantly. I was somewhat appalled, as her husband was definitely not my type. And it wasn't my style to fool around with my friends' men anyway. I just wasn't that desperate.

As the story, would go, the main culprit feeding her the misinformation was my ex-roommate, the one who changed the locks unbeknownst to me. She was the one actually sleeping with the young lady's husband, her so-called best friend, right under the wife's nose. I had no clue, but surprisingly everyone else in graduate school did. It would've been nice if someone had informed me.

Instead of rolling her eyes and distancing herself from me, I wished the wife had come to me like the woman I knew she was and we could have squashed that lie back then. I really liked her. And her aloofness really hurt my feelings. My naivety checked her behavior off as part of her northern abrasiveness. You know how those Northern folk are. Just kidding (Smile).

The life lesson for me was to never put myself in a situation where I'd be dependent on others for my livelihood, especially as an adult. Sometimes when people think you need them, they feel it gives them the right to treat you any kind of way.

Always be aware of your surroundings. If not, like me, you could end up being a part of something that you aren't really a part of. People have gotten killed from less foolishness. But God!

25.
Links

You can't change the family you were born into. They are who they are and do what they do. Unfortunately, their behavior doesn't just affect them, but you too. Links apply to friends and associates alike. Remember, we are linked by choice. If we are not on the same course, it's okay to break the link to swim and not sink. Tired of sinking, drowning?

F

A link is a bind or tie that connects you to someone or something. Think about it. What are you linked to? I'm linked to the bloodline of Jesus! God is the first link, then His son Jesus is the second link, the Holy Spirit is the third link, my great-great grandparents are the fourth link, and so far, and so on.

Now we as a family are linked to the church which takes us back to our first link. Jesus said I will build my church on this rock and the gates of hell shall not prevail against it (Mathew 16:18). I have a very strong link hold on my Lord and Savior Jesus Christ, who is the head of my life. If I did not trust Jesus, all of my links would be disconnected. My bond would be weak and my ties in a knot. Again I say think about it. What are you linked to? I pray you are connected to Jesus, Family and Love.

K

Remember, love is what links us, not blood. Just because a person is a relative, doesn't mean they are related. When a person reveals their true colors, stop pretending not to see the rainbow. They are what I call Jinky-Links. They drain and deplete you; always taking, never giving.

Be cognizant of how people make you feel, family or not. Pay attention to your inner-thermometer, your emotional temperature gauge. If they are sucking the life right out of you, loosen the chain and love them at a distance. You'll know when. It'll get to a point when their mere presence drains your soul. Then, it'll be time to separate for your own welfare.

We are all linked to someone or something. There isn't any mystery to people. They will always show you who they are and what they are about. Our job is to always be alert, listen, and pay attention. See them for who and what they are, not what we hope them to be.

I have a lot of links as I'm sure you do too. Just know who your links are and adjust their closeness depending on their trustworthiness. There is nothing wrong with loving them at a distance. You don't love people just because. That's a misnomer. If they are not trustworthy or keep up a lot of strife in your life, you may not even like them, damn love. And that's okay. They have shown who they are and you must deal with them accordingly.

Somewhere along the way, we've heard the message to accept people as they are and love them unconditionally. My take is the same, but with caution. You have to protect you and yours. Just move their links to a safe distance, away from your heart and checkbook. You are not helping them if they are always dependent on you. Obviously your interference is preventing them from learning their life lesson and growth.

You can pray until your hair turns gray. Behavior will still be a choice. And with every choice, there are consequences. It's life. You can give your all and still they fall. Behavior will still be a choice. You can talk until you're blue and still they'll be fools. Behavior will still be a choice. You can hope for the best and still they'll fail life's simplest test. Behavior will still be a choice. At the end of the day, when there are no words left to say, remember, their behavior is always a choice!

26.
I Am

I am me- happy and free. Look at what I've achieved; the man or woman I've become. I am on my way to greater things. A new day has begun.

F

I am a child of the King. I am saved, sanctified and washed in the blood of Jesus (Acts 2:4). I am a faithful believer that there is only one true and living God who created the universe. I am a nobody, trying to tell everybody, about somebody who will save anybody. I am strong and I don't worry about anything, because I know without a shadow of a doubt, God has my back and "Won't He do it!" I'm a genuine, easy going person, who is responsible, reliable and spontaneous.

I am a Cum Laude graduate of Grambling State University. I have been working for Caddo Parish School Board, on and off, since 1989. I'm in a commercial for Velocity Credit Union. I am in a hair modeling book for

Dudley's Q+ Hair Images, volume 10. I got married first, and then I had my children. I have no tattoos (Leviticus 19:28). I treat everyone with kindness and no one is a stranger to me. I stay in control at all times and I don't let the devil steal my joy. I listen and watch closely to how others handle their devastating situations. If I have a similar one, I'd know how to react with wisdom and patience. I am a faithful, forgiving Christian who really loves the Lord. I am now an author! Hooray!

K

I am a lot of things in a lot of ways on a lot of days. I am journey. I live to learn and grow every day. What about you? Who are you? What good do you do for the betterment of humanity? If you aren't good to yourself, how can you be good to or good for others?

You are what you believe you are. It's reflective in every part of your life. Today is your optimum opportunity to recreate yourself into someone new and exciting. I can honestly say I am happy and complete. I enjoy being me and spending time alone. It allows me to gather my thoughts and perfect my spiritual senses. A lot of people have problems being by themselves. They need people or sound around. Pure silence bothers them.

The universe is vast. There will always be new endeavors to try, experiences to explore. Enjoy you and everything around you will be a joy. I love my life. I wouldn't trade it for anything. It has been good to me even with all its ups and downs. I wouldn't have appreciated the sunshine if it wasn't for the rain.

I hold advanced degrees. Yet, I still love to learn. I awake every morning excited with great expectation. I am so grateful to be in the land of the living. Being alive is my contract with God to do wonderful things for humanity in His name and for His honor. What have you done to better the world lately?

So what we hold titles and positions? At the end of the day, our greatest role should be love. Love is all that matters. Wherever we go, whatever we do, it's imperative that we always are, in the present moment, who God has ordained us to be- love.

Throughout our day, in every way, we are the reflection of God's truth in everything we say and do. We should never be swayed by others' agendas or beliefs. If they aren't aligned with the righteousness of God, we shouldn't participate. Even if it requires us to stand alone, then so be it. I'd rather stand by myself in love, than with others in hate.

I am too old and been around too long not to know right from wrong. So I'm past pettiness. You should be too. If you are still doing the same thing you've done before, you haven't grown. If you are not enthusiastic about being an integral part of something worthwhile for the betterment of humankind, you aren't living up to your God-potential.

There is always something for you and your family to do, to be a part of. What need is in your community? I started a nonprofit in 2014 to help 18-25 year olds get back on track and on a career path. Our team is determinedly anchored in the belief that our young adult population is worth a dime and our time. At their age, they may not need our hugs and kisses, but they definitely need our guidance and direction.

Tina Turner asked, "What's love got to do with it?" I say everything. Everything we say and do should be in the name of love. Give the gift of yourself to better humanity. I know I am a better me because of you.

27.
Lifeline

Many hold special places in my heart. But you, my dear, are the lifeline to my soul. Without you, I feel empty, incomplete. You are my every heartbeat.

F

Lifeline to me means your Savior, someone who can rescue you from a life-threatening situation. My lifeline is, first and foremost, God my heavenly Father (the one and only true living Jehovah); Jesus Christ His son, who shed His blood and died on the cross, went to hell and took back the keys of death from Satan, rose on the third day with all power in his hand for my/our sins; The Holy Spirit, who Jesus left as our comforter, to lead and guide us in the right direction (John 14:26). When we say, something told me not to do that. That something is the Holy Spirit.

My second lifeline is my parents for not aborting me. They kept me, raised me, loved me, nurtured me, blessed me, taught me right from wrong and put the fear of God in me so when I die, I'll be in the bosom of Jesus Christ, my Lord and Savior.

My third lifeline is my two children, who were connected to me via their naval cords at birth. God blessed me with a healthy, loving son. Nineteen and three-forth months later, He blessed me with a beautiful, healthy daughter. I thank God that all of my lifelines are still alive.

K

Love is a wonderful thing. But the direct opposite of love is pain. For everything that is born, one day it must transform (die or crossover). So be grateful now for the time God has allowed you with your loved ones. Tomorrow isn't promised.

I am grateful for good friends and family. Not all of my friends and family are good. Some I just tolerate and I'm sure you do too. It is what it is. No sense in pretending that it's something it's not. Madear used to say, "As long as you know a person, they can't hurt you." It's when we deny the truth inside (ignoring our inner thermostat), we have problems.

I have love-lines to those I love and I love them endlessly. For the purpose of this writing however, I would say my mother would be my lifeline. I don't know what I'd do if I didn't have her in my life. My heart goes out to friends and family who have lost their lifelines. I can only imagine the never yielding heartbreak. Heaven knows, even the kindest words won't fill the hole that's in their souls. So I won't even try.

Growing up, my mother and I had a peculiar relationship. She worked a lot and was often missing in action. Emotionally, she was not there. I don't recall her ever coming to any of my high school functions or ever seeing me march in my high school band. The same held true for college. She probably showed up once or twice.

Over the years, I've heard the horror stories of the violence and abuse my mom had to endure as a child. I soon realized that she had her own private demons to contend with, plus three rambunctious children. She loved us the way she knew how to love us. For that, I am grateful.

I knew instinctively she loved me although she never conveyed it. Parents from my era weren't the touchy-feely types. Their love language was putting a roof over our heads, feeding and clothing us. Anything else, oh well!

As previously mentioned, I almost lost my mother in January, 2015. My family and I were not prepared for another loss. Plus, we had just been in her company and she was fine, being her jovial, hilarious self. Life is funny. In a moment's time, she was knocking at death's door. Thank God the door did not open.

My mom and I have always been close. Now we are best buds. She is my best friend and confidant. I know tomorrow's not promised, so I make a point to spend as much quality time as possible with this grace God has granted me.

A common theme I've heard people echo after losing a loved one is, "I wish I had more time." There's no time like the present. And what you deem as important, your reasons for not spending quality time with loved ones, won't matter a damn after they are gone.

Calendar in love-dates with your special someone. It doesn't have to be a specific occasion. Just because, is fine enough. Two things I would advise you to do, if you haven't already. Insure your loved one (s) and take a CPR class. I have done both. It's nothing worse than being in a position to be someone's lifeline and you're ill-prepared. So keep the love-lines opened to your lifelines.

28.
Forbidden Fruit

Although sin is pleasurable, it's seasonal. We all know right from wrong. But, for this one moment with you, to the depths of hell I'd go just to feel you in my mind, body, and soul. Watch out now!

F

Forbidden fruit to me is a married man or woman, cheating on their spouse. Married men should only be with the one woman, their wife, and vice versa. One way to prevent Aids is if you are with only one partner, and your partner only with you. A man that has a wife should not even be in your face if he has sexual intentions. Other than being your church member, co-working, neighbor, relative, or friend, he should remain in his space.

Married people that go outside of their marriage are insecure, lonely, crazy, or just plain ole sick. Married men usually fool around because of something lacking at home. They always want more. The sex with his wife of many years has become boring, and they are always looking for something different. Those reasons don't make their cheating right. Married people who step out on their spouse, are not only hurting themselves, but their families as well. Stop the madness people. Make love to your own spouse, not everyone else.

K

You touched a very special part of me that people could only dream of. You touched me with your love. It's hard nowadays to find someone to like, let alone love. But every now and then you come across that special someone that you'd lay it all down for. I am sure, like me, you've been here before. A special someone that had a certain savoir faire that made you do a double take, take notice.

Out of respect, I won't reveal the name of my forbidden fruit. That was a different place and time. And we both are with our hearts' desires. With the first meeting of my forbidden fruit, all my senses said yes. I knew I could spend eternity in his arms. His eyes captivated me. His smile warmed me. His character secured me. But his public image cautioned me.

I knew I couldn't and wouldn't masquerade as someone I was not. My mama didn't raise me like that. What you saw is what you got with me, period. If I could accept you as is, then I'd expect the same. If any aspect about me didn't work for you, then set sail, Mister. See ya! I'd give you your oar, paddle along. I wasn't about to put on any airs, or be, in any way, who I was not, and neither should you. You'd eventually hate yourself for being phony, living a lie.

I am a romantic, but there must be something past romanticism. I don't believe that there is such a thing as love at first sight. It may be lust at first glance, but definitely not love. Love is built upon respect and trust, the foundational principles of any relationship. You can't love a person you don't know and you can't know a person you just met. You have to test the relationship. Only time and situational events will assess its strength and authenticity.

Like I said before, my forbidden fruit was a man of success and power, not so much privilege. At least, he didn't start out that way. His achievements were hard earned and I admired that. Like most people, I love a story of triumph. However, I knew he needed someone more prim and proper than me; eye-candy perhaps, a polished trophy. And I was and still am far from the bourgeoisie type.

Back then, my attire consisted of blue jeans, flip flops and a baseball cap. I was never comfortable wearing a dress or high heel shoes. I walked with a mission and the tomboy in me wouldn't allow me to sit like a lady with my legs closed or crossed. I still sit gap-legged today. As a result, I hardly wear dresses.

Regarding make-up and hair, they weren't priorities then and still aren't today. It wasn't uncommon for my girlfriends to give me a hairdo or dress-over. I never saw what all the fuss was about anyway. If a man wanted you, he wanted you, not the superficial fluff.

Note I said what a man wanted, not a boy. Boys like playing with toys and I wasn't a game to be played. Hell, as long as I had on clean underwear, I was ready to go. Thus, my fetish for lingerie. I might've looked like a hobo/tomboy on the outside but underneath, I had on nice undergarments. Just my girl thing! Some girls liked purses, shoes, clothes, etc. Mine was undies.

As I've gotten older, I've upgraded some, not much. I am thankful for friends and family that accept me as I am. It takes too much time and energy for me to get dolled up. Past 8:00 p.m. it's a done deal anyway. I am fast asleep. (Laugh)

Regarding my forbidden fruit, I knew I couldn't live up to an image. I also knew I couldn't dumb myself down. I had to be me. My life demanded it. So I let him live his dream, which didn't require me not living mine. Like Kenny Rogers said, "You have to know when to fold, let go, walk away, or run."

My humble advice is before you pick fruit from any vineyard; know exactly what you are getting and the expectation. Look at the roots. See how it grows. Know what it will take to nourish it.

You may discover that your chosen fruit may not be to your liking and that's okay, especially if it requires a lot of pruning. Like me, you may have to leave it to flourish in someone else's vineyard.

29.
Turn Back the Hands of Time

If we could turn back the hands of time, we all would do things differently. Then life wouldn't hold this big mystery. But we can't. So, let's make the best of what is and live!

F

If I could turn back the hand of time, I would let Pastor Lester Summerall lay hands on me and pray. My mom said when he laid hands on her; she really fell down in the Spirit without being forced. I had the opportunity to experience being slain in the Spirit but I didn't go up when called. I would wait until I was married before being sexually active. If you have relations with everyone you date before you are married....That's not good! That's how you can get hurt, confused, pregnant, talked about, diseased, and only God knows what else. So wait patiently on your own mate. It's better to marry than burn (I Corinthians 7:9).

Another thing, if I could turn back the hand of time, I would have gone into the United States Air Force, made a career of it and retired in twenty or thirty years! Right about now, I would be relaxing by my pool, with a cool refreshing colorful drink, while my retirement was being deposited into my savings account, collecting interest.

K

I have learned so much on this journey called life. In hindsight, I probably would have done a few things differently. But I wonder, with any life alteration, would I still be the person I am? I think life's trials have made me stronger, wiser and more loving. For that reason alone, I wouldn't change a thing. Would I alter, tweak an area or two? I'm sure I would.

First, I'd probably start with taking school more seriously. My parents didn't participate much in my secondary education so I never valued doing my best. I'd do just enough to get by. Thus, I got out of middle and high school what I put in, not much. Plus, the trauma of experiencing my grandmother's death in the house fire didn't help either. It was hard for me to connect the dots afterwards in comprehension, retention, and speech.

College was different, however. I graduated Cum Laude. I guess I was a little older and wiser.

I was rather shy and timid growing up. I wanted everyone to like me and every stranger was a friend. I had to learn the hard way that people don't always have your best interest at heart, including family and friends. The fact that they are in your immediate circle means they have closer access to your heart. Be smart. Monitor your inner-thermo. If it tells you to be aware, it's done its job. Our failure to take heed means certain situations are sure to repeat.

You may ask why I am echoing this point throughout my writings. It's because I know firsthand; and truth be told, you do too. Just because you are close to a person, doesn't mean they won't hurt you. Remember Jinky-Links- attachments that jink our lives with all kinds of knots and kinks.

We are all connected and need one another. When our paths cross, and they will, if we don't have strong constitutions, we will always be tossed here and there, off on destinations that aren't ours to travel. Or, silently consenting by doing nothing and ignoring the truth.

Now that I'm older, I realize that I should have stood up for myself more, letting my voice be heard. It probably wouldn't have altered the situation in any way, but it would've changed me for the better. It would have given me a voice and a choice. And that's what life is all about.

By doing nothing, I allowed the wrong to persist which was an error. Oh but when you know better, you do better!

Of course, I would've also gotten grief counseling early on. I believe experiencing my grandmother's death changed who I was and who I'd become for years to come. She was my other mother. So losing her was like losing a part of me that's taken me a lifetime to get over. And you never really do.

I would have married my husband sooner and probably had children, ahhh! The latter being a big probably. Although we love children and were blessed to raise our great nephew, our life is whole and complete with just us. We have learned to play the hand we were dealt. Some may disagree. No argument here. Not having biological children didn't make us any less of a man or a woman. Just because you can make a baby doesn't make you a parent.

Lastly, I probably would have been more adventurous, taking more chances. The fear of failure kept me close to my comfort zone. But now, I'm coming out of my self-imposed nest, ready and willing to explore new heights and depths. Join me. Won't you? Why don't you?

30.
The Game

Some say life is a game. You must know the rules of engagement if you want to play with the big boys. Unfortunately, we don't live in a utopian society. And of course, everyone doesn't play fair. So, pin up your hair, roll up your sleeves and get in the game of life to play to win!

F

I never was much on playing games because I'm the type of person who likes to keep it real. I love to joke around and make people laugh, especially people I barely know. But I will play a game or two if it's in my favor. By my being so nice and naïve, I never wanted to hurt anyone's feelings. So, for example, if a person wanted something from me and I knew it was immoral, I'd pretend as if I didn't understand what they were asking.

For instance, back in high school, one of my teachers tried to rap to me. I was in the 9th grade, still wearing pony tails, dresses with ruffles above my knee caps, with matching socks and tennis shoes. Sometimes I even wore hi-water pants. Now that I look back, I was still playing with baby dolls too. Hey, I was only 14! I hadn't even had my period yet.

This teacher used to bring me gifts at school. On one occasion, he brought me sinus pills when I was sick, and gave me a quick smack on the lips to help me feel better. He was a very fine, well-built married man with a child. I wondered what he wanted with my skinny, flat-chested self. I guess I was leading him on by accepting his gifts. But at 14, I didn't really know any better. Nonetheless, nothing ever transpired between us. Years later, he ended up divorcing his wife and marrying one of my classmates. I never said a word. I knew at a young age that I had to play the game.

K

I think it's a sin not to educate children about the evils of the world, allowing them to grow up thinking all is fair in love and war. And we all know that is far from the truth. Everyone should be allowed to make mistakes, feel the agony of a heartbreak, loss, or disappointment without judgment, and be able to check it off to life and move on.

Too often we get stuck paying penance for a childhood, teenage, or young adult indiscretion that a lifetime won't heal. The adage, "with age comes wisdom," isn't totally true. The saying should be "keep living, you'll get some sense one way or another." And as long as you live, there will always be life lessons to learn.

It was my first job out of graduate school. I had arrived, so I thought. I made it- the first in my nucleus family to graduate from college. I wore the crown of success on my chest.

It was the late eighties; George H. Bush was President. From day one, I realized that being educated wouldn't be enough. I somehow had to prove to the non-blacks that I was better than the negative imagery being showcased across media outlets. Every television station must've used the same mug shot of the black male. I would cringe at every crime announced on T.V. because I knew I was being subliminally judged by my counterparts.

With those of my same ancestry, I felt a need to dumb myself down with some of them, as not to appear better than they were in any form or fashion. God forbid I bought something of value, then eyes would roll and distancing would occur. I could feel it. And like a dummy, I went along with it just to be in the pack of my cultural social club.

From my family, I could never rise higher than their impression of me. No matter what, I was still Little Mil from Stoner Hill. True, but a bit more wiser and knowledgeable. My family kept it real, telling it like it was whether I liked it or not. I had to always be on my Ps and Qs, making sure I carried the family banner with pride. Like all families, you had those who fell by the wayside and stayed there. Although not perfect, I love them the same and wouldn't take anything for them.

It took me time to learn not to internalize the insecurities of some and arrogances of others. Those were their issues, not mine. I applaud everyone's success, absorbing as much knowledge as I can. They inspire me and I plan to join them at the top.

Now that I'm older, I realize that God only created one race of people- the human race. All the other foolishness that exists in the world is not of God, and I refuse to participate in it. I have come to realize that people's ways are just their ways; right, wrong, or indifferent. God, however, requires me to be loving and kind to all mankind. And that's how I'm living.

Even with the state of affairs in the world today, I'm calm knowing who I am, in love and whose I am, in peace. I am God's! This world is the Lord's and the fullness thereof (I Corinthians 10:26). God got us! It's good to watch the news but don't become inundated with all the negativity. Guard what enters your heart, mind, and Spirit.

And for heaven's sake, don't perseverate on it day and night. It will consume you and change you.

Intentionally surround yourself with intelligent, positive people, regardless of their race. If all you know is who you know, then you haven't grown. You learn by obtaining knew information, not holding on to outdated knowledge and beliefs. Never try to brake, erase, or deem as a mistake that which God created. People don't have to look or sound like me to be accepted. The mere fact that God chose them to share this time and space with me, is a blessing and honor. My inner-thermo tells me this is the way of God and that works for me!

31.
The First

The first time you became aware of your life-altering experience, what happened? Did it change you? Are you better or worse because of it? You are still here so it didn't take you out. What were the life lessons you learned?

F

The first spirit in this universe is God, then Jesus. The first time you meet someone is the most memorable of all. The first day of school is sort of scary. At age twelve, my first tongue kiss was unacceptable. At youth camp, Johnny stuck his tongue in my mouth and I snapped my teeth closed to try to block it. Yuck, I thought to myself....that's gross!

My first time at a wrestling match, I saw blood come out of the man's head and everyone screamed, "Get him, get him!" I was about 7 years old at the time, and said to myself, while my stomach was turning from seeing the blood, "How could my daddy bring me to a place like this!?"

If you are the first one to finish a race, that usually means you're the fastest. If you finish your work first, you're the quickest. If you complete your test first, you're the smartest. First means #1, Uno in Spanish! Most people want to be the first to accomplish a task so they can be recognized and famous. But the bible says, "The first shall be last, and the last first" (Matthew 19:30). Just remember, your first impression is an everlasting one.

K

I believe if we are breathing, life is teaching. We are always students of life. So why get angry with a new lesson? My first "real" kiss was in high school. Okay, I was a late bloomer. Yes, I kissed boys before. Either I didn't know what I was doing or they were amateurs, but when I kissed Geraldo, I felt it in my toes (Laugh). We were in Byrd's High School marching band together and sat by one another on the band bus. For four years, everywhere the band traveled, Geraldo and I were seat-mates, rather kissing mates. Our favorite kissing candy- Jolly Ranchers, apple flavored.

I had a high school first-love. Or, at least I thought I did. He eventually dumped me for a cheerleader. I had another crush on an upper classman, but he had a crush on someone else. Bummer! And so were the high school days.

Later, I met a cutie named Orlando, who attended Fair Park, a rival high school. He had the most beautiful smile. He even bought me a promise ring, ahhh. Fast forward several years. While attending college at Grambling State University, I discovered that dear ole Orlando had several girlfriends back in high school and bought each of us promise rings (Laugh). Today, many of us are lifelong friends because of Orlando, primarily Felicia and I. We have been college best friends for over 30 years. Thanks, Orlando!

None of my young loves ever materialized. Like the ocean, emotions moved like waves then, back and forth. One day you are in love, the next in like, the next in hate. Regardless of your age, a heartbreak of any kind still hurts like hell. When you are older, you are just better able to deal with it and put it into perspective. Well, at least most of us can.

What you live through, you don't have to continue to go through. **F**eel, **d**eal and **h**eal (FDH) so you can go on and live strong. Keep living, you'll eventually become a master at handling your feelings and dealing with the upheavals of relationships. It's life, like day and night.

Geraldo and Orlando have since gone on to glory. Both of my childhood friends left this earth too soon. But they'll forever be firsts in my heart.

32.
Regrets

How would you ever know what feels good if you've never had bad? How would you ever know what works if things didn't go awry? Regret is an emotion that propels you towards excellence if you channel it right. Look at regret as an opportunity to reset. What doesn't change, remains the same.

F

I regret certain times when I should have spoken up, but instead I stayed silent. I regret times I should have stayed silent, but I opened my big mouth. I regret the times I drank too much and felt nauseated afterwards, until I threw up and felt better. I regret the times I committed sin, prayed to the Lord I would never do it again, but did it again and again anyway.

I regret the times when I used profanities when my children wouldn't listen or when someone made me angry. I have control over that now. I regret that I'm not retiring from a job after 20+ years like lots of my friends and relatives are doing. But I'm still searching for that great job to retire from soon.

I regret the times I wanted to do something, but fear stopped me. Not anymore! God does not give us a spirit of fear but a sound mind (II Timothy 1:7).

K

I would imagine that we all have some type of regret. I sometimes wonder what my life would be like if this or that had or had not occurred. So if I had to do an honest-inventory, I would probably have a few re-dos in certain areas of my life.

One regret for sure, would be my heavy involvement in religion growing up. To say it was cult-like, would be an understatement. Back then, people were religious fanatics, condemning and judging all who didn't align with their belief systems to hell. This was the culture of the bible churches I attended, the fire and brimstone mentality.

I believe I missed out on certain life experiences, rites of passage, being too afraid to sin or terrified to fail. I would beat myself up for any mistake or indiscretion, even if it was just in thought. The church followed suit every Sunday by telling me how no good and unworthy I was, as a filthy rag (Isaiah 64:6).

I consider myself spiritual now, not religious. I love God and see things in a different light. I don't believe God sweats the small stuff church-folk bicker and complain over. I feel the church has an unhealthy control over God's people which makes trying to live righteously a bore and a chore.

God is love and He created us in His image- love. You may disagree. However, if being low-down, cursed from your mother's womb works for you, no argument here. I can accept differences of opinions without feeling a need to banish your soul to hell or start a religious war. I'm just saying.

To me, God is more than a book, building made with hands, or traditions of man. He lives in the hearts and souls of His children. He is love. Love is what I purpose to be. What about you? What God do you serve? I pray the God of love.

33.
Reflection

You are a reflection of all your life experiences- the good, the bad and the OMG! What do others see when they look at you? Your reflection tells your truth.

F

As I look back over my life, I can truly say I had an awesome one! God, our Father has been the head of my life as long as I can remember. I have God-sent parents who raised me to be a respectable, God-fearing young lady. I had awesome grandparents who taught me right from wrong and how not to date cheap guys. At a very young age, my Big Mama talked to me about the birds and the bees. She told me to keep my dress down and pants up! Still, as a child, there were unfortunate situations in which older boys touched me inappropriately. I never told my parents, until this writing.

As I continue to reflect, one of the greatest life lessons I've learned was that if you play with fire, you'll get burned. Also, not to allow others to dictate to you who you are, because if you do, that's what you'll eventually become. The main lesson I've learned in life, was that you reap what you sow (Galatians 6:7).

As adults, I feel we should teach young ladies, as well as pre-teens, not to fall for the same old okey-doke behind a man. First, let a man be a man. But more importantly, let him be a gentleman. He should always respect you, open the car door for you, and speak to you in a decent manner. He should also honor your parents as well as his. A man should not be borrowing your car, money or shacking at your house. And of course, he should never cheat on you or put his hands on you.

Lastly, this writing has been a great experience, co-writing with my College BFF, Kamilah. It has afforded me the opportunity to reminisce over my past and see how good God has been to me. I am more than a conqueror and my future awaits me. Yours does as well! Keep the faith!

K

People hear what you say, but believe what you do. I have done a lot in my life. Some things I'm proud of, other things I'm not. But for the most part, I am truly thankful for the grace God's given me, chances beyond measure.

Writing this book has been therapeutic to me on so many levels. I've been able to close old doors, address old scars, forgive old infractions and revisit old acquaintances. It has also brought to light my need to let go of parasitic relationships that don't support my best life. I respectfully refer to them as Jinky-Links. You can't live with them. And, you don't know what your life would be without them. Some friends and family you have to love at a distance, but still love them just the same.

Sometimes you have to hear your thoughts spoken on paper to realize how blessed you are and how much your friends and family mean to you. Felicia and I, along with another girlfriend started this journey in May, 2015. But only Felicia and I stayed the course. And we finished, finished, finished! Praise God!

What's funny is that Felicia and I did the same thing over thirty years ago in college. We started out together at eighteen years of age as freshmen. We would study and finish class projects together, not allowing the other to outdo the other (healthy competition). If I wanted to hang-out and knew Felicia was in the dormitory studying, I would change my plans and vice versa.

We began college in the Fall, 1982 and both graduated Cum Laude with our Bachelor's Degree in Criminal Justice Fall, 1986, committed to staying the course until completion. Although we are different on so many fronts, we are both children of God and love people, friends, and family; wishing nothing less than God's very best for them.

As I reflect over my life and where I've come from, I am truly grateful. I don't know where I'd be if I couldn't have shared this space and time with you. We are one. You are an important part of me. In you I breathe and see the brightness of tomorrow.

I am so inspired and refreshed by humanity that I cheer and celebrate with every expression of love shown in the world. Sure there are issues. It's impossible not to have them with man's ego-need for power, greed, and control. But I see what I strive to be- love. And, so be it in my mind, body and soul!

Life is better than good, so live your life to the fullest holding nothing back. You are more than your hips, lips, eyes and thighs or life's myths and lies. You have grace on your side. Be open to change and growth. Welcome new discoveries and you'll find infinite possibilities. Be the change you want the world to be. I have started with me and await your company.

Made in the USA
Lexington, KY
07 January 2017